# SPELLS
## FOR
# CHANGE

# SPELLS
## FOR
# CHANGE

### A GUIDE FOR MODERN WITCHES

## FRANKIE
## CASTANEA

Andrews McMeel
PUBLISHING®

Andrews McMeel Publishing
a division of Andrews McMeel Universal
1130 Walnut Street, Kansas City, Missouri 64106

www.andrewsmcmeel.com

*Spells for Change* was originally published in the UK in 2021
by The Orion Publishing Group Ltd.

23 24 25 26 27 TEN 10 9 8 7 6 5 4 3 2

ISBN: 978-1-5248-7163-5

Library of Congress Control Number: 2021949168

ATTENTION: SCHOOLS AND BUSINESSES

Andrews McMeel books are available at quantity discounts with
bulk purchase for educational, business, or sales promotional use.
For information, please e-mail the Andrews McMeel Publishing Special
Sales Department: sales@amuniversal.com.

To my parents, whose belief in me never faltered.

# CONTENTS

# INTRODUCTION

Within the modern witch's world, there is virtually no aspect or topic unavailable to the inquisitive reader. From Wicca to green witchcraft and information on folk and herbal magick, the amount of literature and resources available to new witches is endless. However, most of the beginner books that I could get my hands on when I first started my craft around six or seven years ago were based around the Wiccan religion, or particularly whitewashed, covering up the history and culture of voices of color. I found that there were specific books on certain paths, like green witchcraft or hedge witchcraft, but no book that gave a starting point without the influence of another source or religion. I felt like the information available to those who wanted to pursue their own path was limited, and there was a basic foundation for learning about witchcraft that wasn't being shared.

This was around 2015 or 2016. Since that point, more books have emerged that approach witchcraft as a practice formulated to the individual which are less ritualistic and ceremonial. Although ritual, ceremony, and traditional witchcraft have their places in the modern witch's world, more and more witches are finding their way to the Craft and looking for noncommittal places to start. Some argue that the path of the witch is sacred, and should be kept under close lock and key, and only those who can commit to years of training and initiation deserve the title. I take a different approach in this book.

*Spells for Change: A Guide for Modern Witches* covers what I, a practicing eclectic/folk witch, consider the basic foundations of spellcraft and formulating your practice. Eclecticism describes a practice that picks and chooses from many open traditions of witchcraft to create a customized version, while folk witchcraft describes, very simply, a magick of the people emphasized by use of the items of the land and the materials around them. This is the book I wish I'd had at sixteen, when I started researching my craft—it is devoid of a particular path or religion and fully adaptable to what works best for you and your craft. All of the spells are lifted from my own practice, and each section is devoted to looking at these foundations of manifesting change through spell work, intent, and mindfulness with a decolonized point of view (see page 180). These are methods that are tried and true to me, and have been backed by my experience in my practice, by other books, and by my mentors and friends who are witches. This book strives to take into consideration accessibility and different learning abilities, and to bring awareness to the origin of the Craft—its history of appropriation and colonization, and how we, as witches, can use witchcraft as a form of activism as well as a vessel for change.

We, as modern witches, are not only living through a rebirth of the Craft but a rapidly changing world. When a many-thousand-year-old practice focused on rebalancing the power of the universe, connecting with yourself, and connecting with the divine is brought into the modern day, how does it change? How does it morph and adapt to fit the tech-savvy, capitalist world of today? How do materialism, classism, racism, and power dynamics affect our practice? How do we carve time not just for ourselves to reconnect with the universe but time for empathy and the will to create a better world?

This book is created to add nuance to a practicing witch's craft and create a starting place for those looking to begin, but also to allow those who have never heard of the Craft to explore it in theory. What is it? How do we use it? It discusses the tools that are used, the history of witchcraft, the love and prioritization of self, and so much more. As more individuals find witchcraft, more questions will arise, but my goal is to assess and answer all the questions that I have so far received while building an online social media platform and being a mentor as a modern-day practicing witch.

# PART 1

# WHAT DOES IT MEAN
# TO BE A
# MODERN WITCH?

# WHO ARE THE MODERN-DAY WITCHES?

Far away from the long, hooked noses of *Hocus Pocus* and the power-hungry Nancy in *The Craft* lives a very different type of witchcraft. Often, media interpretations of witchcraft, and what a witch is, have helped to demonize the term. Where *Harry Potter* and *Chilling Adventures of Sabrina* paint scenes of levitation, contracts with the devil, and wand waving, real witchcraft is very different. Many trace the origins of witchcraft and their first discussions on it to the Salem witch trials of the seventeenth century; however, its roots are actually much older. Witchcraft is based in many ancient pagan traditions where shamans, priests/priestesses, Druids, and oracles were seen as holy. It can be found in the Celtic lands in closed Irish practices (see page 180), handed down from generation to generation; among the Romani peoples; in different parts of Italy; and so much more. Some may define witchcraft in more traditional, ritualistic terms but others may find that witchcraft is as simple as giving intent and meaning to a daily activity, honoring a deity through action, or being aware of the energy of the universe and how it influences what we bring forth into our lives. The idea of manipulating energy, calling on a spirit, using herbs, candles, and good-luck charms to sway life one way or another is ancient, and has infiltrated the modern day in more ways than one. Knocking on wood and other superstitions descended from folk magic, much like blowing out birthday candles comes from the idea that our movement and breath hold life, energy, and power.

A common misconception about witchcraft is that it includes worship of the devil, when in reality, without the intertwining with another religion, it's about reclaiming your power and refining your identity. Most witches don't believe in or subscribe to the Abrahamic beliefs of monotheism, hell, or the devil, and those among us who do believe don't typically seek those entities out. Those who do work with the "devil" don't tend to work with the Christian devil but rather a different form of that entity from the perspective of Satanism or Luciferian magick. Some witches are Wiccan, a modern pagan tradition surrounding a god and goddess, or they look to the ancient pantheons—Greek, Norse, Egyptian, Celtic—for guidance. All of these religions and paths have different traditions and ideas surrounding divinity, none of which are inherently tied to witchcraft. There are also Christian, Muslim, and Jewish witches, who devote their craft and workings to their God. Some witches are atheist or agnostic, commonly referred to as secular, where the gods are seen less as divine and more as aspects of nature. Almost all witches have close ties to nature and communicate with the universe in some aspects, whether that's a specific deity, the higher self, or just all the energy that is and that will be.

Witchcraft, in itself, is a broad term. It encapsulates, at its core, one who practices the Craft. Although its foundations are highly debated, the Craft is casting spells to create an outcome. However, beyond this, witchcraft is so much more—it is not a miracle worker but rather a tool to use alongside our day-to-day lives. It's not a solution but rather an aid.

Witchcraft is rooted in the idea that all human beings contain energy—neither bad nor good—that can be harnessed and sent out to the universe with intent to create a specific outcome. Sounds simple, but the process of finding, balancing, and connecting not only to your energy but to the energy of the universe (sometimes referred to as "spirit" or the "higher self") is a process that encourages the individual to challenge what they believe, push their limits, and prod at their darkest aspects of self. Through the many veins of witchcraft, spells are approached in different ways—through meditation, use of candles, ointments, and herbs, or secured in jars and buried to let the spirit do with it what it will.

If you're looking to find a traditional and historical account of how the esoteric, occult, and the Craft have been used throughout the ages, I suggest *Traditional Witchcraft: A Cornish Book of Ways* by Gemma Gary, as well as *The Secret Teachings of All Ages* by Manly P. Hall. *Traditional Witchcraft* discusses witchcraft of British origin and brings forward wonderful points about what traditional witchcraft looked like, and how it can be changed to fit the modern day. *The Secret Teachings of All Ages* works as an encyclopedia for the esoteric, collecting philosophies, different mysticisms, and practices from all over the historical world in a compendium of information.

The foundation of witchcraft is laid in many ways, including studies of meditation, grounding, mani-festation, cleansing, protection, banishing, and binding—all terms you will become familiar with as this book progresses. Each type of study has both personal and worldwide applications, whether it's protecting the home or self from negative energies through boundaries and charms, or binding a harmful person to help a friend. Each brings you closer to creating change within yourself, the environment around you, and the society we live in, and closer to a greater awareness of the universe and the different energies that exist within it.

As the practice of modern witchcraft becomes more socially acceptable and widespread, we don't just have to look at its exceedingly metaphysical and spiritual sides. The more mundane and basic aspects of the Craft are just as important as the more complex practices such as astral projection and intense spell work. Witchcraft is the care and prioritization of self, the upkeep of mental health, and the appreciation of the world around you.

Witchcraft is also personal. Every practice is different, and not every witch has a coven—another common trope among the media. Many witches prefer solitary practice, which is where they conduct rituals and spells by themselves. A plethora of different lanes of witchcraft exist with different focuses. Green witchery and hedge witchery are focused on herbalism and nature, while kitchen witchery focuses on incorporating magick and spell work into cooking. There are folk witches, often described as the "magick of the people," who are categorized by their use of the elements and materials around them or their adherence to long-standing traditions. Solitary witches are those who practice alone, and secular witches work like atheist witches, within a less spiritual framework and using things that are not overtly religious. Eclectic witches pull from varying open paths to create an effective practice, and all witches use different tools like crystals, tarot cards, and herbs to construct a practice.

Just as a witch doesn't need to rush into advanced magicks to be powerful, they don't need to define their practice right away. I consider myself an eclectic neopagan witch, which took years to pin down and is still considered a broad set of terms within the pagan and witch community. I've tried to study and learn about everything under the sun, and I often encourage new witches to do the same. Even if you're worried that kitchen witchery or a coven may not be for you, spend some time looking into it and learning about it to make sure. After six or so years in practice, I am still learning about new things every day—and will be for the rest of my life. Witches need a curiosity and willingness to grow and change, sometimes completely and sometimes in minuscule ways, for the entirety of their journey in the Craft. I've found my strengths in divination, particularly intuitive tarot reading, protection magick, and working and communing with deities and higher-level entities. Although that sounds like a lot, it is tiny in comparison to the scope and sheer amount of knowledge available on the different practices, paths, and methods of spell casting. Learning and exploring different paths of the craft does not necessarily mean that you have to follow that path, temporarily or permanently, and I have known many witches who pulled a 180 and completely changed their practice partway through their journey.

The important part of this is that although each practice is unique and personal to every witch, down to the way they cast spells, each path must be approached with respect. There are certain practices that aren't even open to the majority of practitioners, and you may be turned away while trying to learn more. Looking into cultural appropriation and colonization within the modern-day witchcraft community will also give you an understanding of why not taking from closed practices is so important. It's completely possible and extremely important to create a personal practice while still being respectful of those that are not open to you. Decolonization of the Craft and activism with regard to witchcraft are discussed more on page 180.

Modern-day witches are a culmination of the old and new—they travel to the grocery store, work nine-to-fives, and teach in our classrooms. They carry black tourmaline and quartz, and wave bay and rosemary bundles over their doorways. Within an ancient sacred practice, a new generation of witches is rising; those who understand the power of action sided with energy and intent, who fight for the best versions of themselves through whispered chants and candlelight and match their activism with manifestation. The modern witch creates change within the hearth, the heart, and the world, one spell at a time.

# PART 2

# THE TOOLS AND FOUNDATIONS FOR MAKING CHANGE

# THE BASIS OF SPELLCRAFT

**B**efore stepping into spell work as a new witch, it's important to understand the anatomy of a spell. Its foundation is constructed of the following things:

+ **Focus**
   What aspect of your life is this spell focusing on?

+ **Intent/desired goal**
   What do you want to achieve with this spell?

+ **Materials**
   What materials would best help you bring about the goal of this spell?

Depending on the magnitude of the intent you are approaching, different spells need different things. Some spells need only your intent, and many argue that you can practice witchcraft with no materials whatsoever. This works brilliantly for personal spells (although I like using materials in any situation) and can be something as small as daily affirmations to help you become more comfortable and confident in yourself. If you're practicing spells you hope will have bigger effects, like justice spells (see page 187), you may need certain materials and a certain quantity of them to bring about the full change.

The materials we use in spells are important. Every herb, stone, candle color and shape, and oil has particular metaphysical properties and meanings. Oregano is fantastic for bringing in joy, so I often use this herb in my housewarming and protection spells. Amethyst and rose quartz have wonderful healing energy, and specific candle colors and shapes are good for different spells. However, materials without the practitioner are just that—materials. Oregano by itself won't protect a home, and a green candle burned without a thought paired with it can't bring in much wealth. The most important foundation for your craft is you, the practitioner.

Before casting any spell, you have to understand your own energy and the energy of the world around you. Every aspect of nature and self contains power, from the trees to the sea, from the hands to the feet. The elements of nature around us influence our own self, the cycles of the moon and tide, the destruction and creation of fire, and the stabilizing roots of every tree. We can learn different things from different parts of nature, and call on different aspects of it to help us do our workings, like calling upon the elements to assist in casting a circle (see page 77) or using the cycles of the moon to plan for specific spells (see page 96). Certain herbs can be used in spells to match intent and some practitioners even meditate with their herbs and crystals or pray over them to better connect with them before spell work. Ask the moon for guidance when seeking help with change in the cycles of life, or the sun for help when you need assistance with seeing the light. Ask the rivers for help with going with the tide, and sea creatures for help with understanding ebb and flow.

Even your own thoughts have the power to bring change (or stagnancy) into your life. For example, the way you think about yourself influences those you draw into your life. Your hidden fears and flaws will often be mirrored in close relationships. The life cycles that are present in every living thing are seen in the cycles of the moon and seasons. Understanding your energy, including your flaws and fears, as well as the cycles you approach and explore through life, is fundamental to understanding how to manifest change within your life and on a global scale.

To start to understand your own energy, consider the beating of your heart. Much like the ocean tide, our blood ebbs and flows. We take oxygen in, turn it into fuel, and breathe carbon dioxide out. If you are having trouble connecting with your energy, try finding the core of your being.

Sit outside with a candle, or some crystals, and let yourself stand, sit, or lie in the grass. Feel the way it tickles your feet. Listen to your breathing, the wind, the way everything ebbs and flows. With your inhale, imagine breathing in all that is. Imagine all the energy of the universe collecting around your ribcage, swirling around your lungs. With your exhale, imagine casting it outward. Not forcefully, just enough so you get comfortable with the idea of releasing energy via exhalation. This, when matched with intent, can be used as a basic form of spellcraft. No materials, just you, a spot in nature, your breath, and your intent. Start with something small, like a wish, want, or obsessive thought, and let it formulate and grow when you inhale. Become aware of its nature, and why it is present.

When you exhale, imagine giving this want, wish, or thought up to the universe. Let it be carried away with the breeze.

A simple spell that I've always enjoyed is writing a wish on a bay leaf, and burning it. When you understand how we can put power in words, in breath, or in our own energy with intent, you can more fully understand how spells work, and, furthermore, the way the energy of the universe and magick systems work. Your energy and intent are fused together, then carried by the means of your choice—an element, such as fire, spirit, burial, so on and so forth—to the universe to be carried out and returned back to you.

As you continue on in your practice, this can become a form of worship in itself—referred to as animism. However, you may end up finding that the parts of nature you connected with most have direct ties to your patron deities—similarly if you choose the pagan path—which are deities that hold patronage over the individual and remain as lifelong teachers. I always had a connection with cats, and later on Freyja, the Norse goddess of love and war (whose sacred animal is cats), presented herself as an important deity to my practice. Some practitioners find the energy in every living thing to be something worth worship without a title, and some will find that they work better with a specific deity. At the end of the day, all atoms end up as atoms and where you turn to for guidance is a choice you make by yourself.

Once you become familiar with your energy, turn to what you feel like you need and can bring in with spell work. Spells are tools, ways to focus our energy and project it into the void to achieve a particular goal.

I often ask myself the following questions as I'm formulating a spell:

✝ What is the goal of this spell?

✝ Can I achieve this goal without the use of spell work?

✝ Does this spell tamper with forces and things that make the spell so it will backfire easily? For example:
- Free will
- Weather
- Celestial forces, such as spells to influence deities, demons, planets, or higher beings

✝ Does this spell bring me closer to my higher self and/or serve the higher good? For example, are you doing the spell for petty reasons like proving a point or serving your ego, or are you genuine in your intent and feel this will benefit you and/or others?

✝ Is the price or cost of this spell one I am willing to pay?

✝ Do I have the energy and training to complete this spell?

✝ Is this spell one that I am willing to spend my energy and time on?

If my answer to most of these questions is no, I tend to wait to complete the spell. Since we treat spell work as a tool rather than the be-all and end-all, looking into whether the goal can be completed without casting is always imperative. As a practitioner, even if I believe that I can accomplish the goal without casting, I do like to cast something to cover all my bases and ensure success. One of the things often not talked about within witchcraft is that all spell work, even right-hand ("light") spell work, requires a price. The price of the spell depends on the kind of spell. Sometimes this price is energy, a falling-out with a toxic friend, or an opportunity taken away from someone else. This is not a statement to sway you away from the Craft but rather to be mindful—not just in spell casting but everyday life. Newton's third law, "Every action has an equal and opposite reaction," is one that I like to keep in mind in both the mundane and magickal realms. Your choices and energy create a ripple like throwing a stone into a pond, and we can't always be sure how that ripple comes to fruition. I see this not as a way to live through fear and guilt, worrying that my actions will somehow take away something from someone else, but rather I use it as a tool to be mindful, in my spell work and everyday life, of my energy and how it interacts with others.

It's important to be specific about your intent, but, even then, there is a chance that the most clear, well-meaning spell could cause a manifestation that affects others. This does not inherently make spell work bad but rather something to take seriously and think about before casting. If you cast a spell for getting hired for a specific job, you may be taking the job away from someone else who may need it more. If you cast a self-love spell, it may require the ending of a relationship with someone you love, but who could be holding you back from your full potential. Even then, there are certain forces that should not be tampered with—higher forces, such as deities, demons, and celestial bodies, contain power and attempting to influence them with human will simply does not work. Some higher beings can easily take offense at this kind of petty ritual, interpreting it as disrespect, and this may cause them to retaliate. Though this is uncommon, there are sections of mythology devoted to allegory about humans not knowing their place next to gods.

Even the weather is a force to avoid tampering with—Mother Nature and science have their own patterns and ways. Spells done for petty reasons, or as ways of serving the ego, like proving a point or retaliating because someone said something mean about you, have more room to backfire. A strong purpose is needed to cast, and oftentimes the universe, higher self, or even deities—another word for gods and goddesses—if you work with them, may realize that your spell is a waste of energy or not serving your greater good. Some things are not meant to be changed, and because spell work requires an immense amount of energy it's important not to waste it on situations that are not worth your time. Spell work, and the decision to cast a spell, is ultimately deciding whether the part of your life you wish to influence is one you want to change, even if it means a rocky road to that goal. These questions are imperative to the foundation of spell work, as they make you more aware of the root of your desires and goals and what part of your self they ultimately serve.

Another important foundation to spell work is patience— knowing that not everything is meant to be learned immediately and that not all spells will take hold in the timeframe that you want. One of my hardest lessons as a growing witch was that although you may cast a spell, it may not manifest in the way you want, or take hold in the timeframe you expected. Some spells are not in your best interests, like trying to summon back a toxic ex, or are blocked by doubt and never come to fruition. In the same vein, not all spells and workings can be done right away. Practitioners of different cultures and practices sometimes spend upward of a decade waiting until they attempt certain magicks, and there is always more to learn. Don't rush to complete something complicated in order to feel more advanced. The curiosity and drive that you have will help you learn and continue learning for the rest of your journey, but without the basics and a fundamental understanding of witchcraft and spell casting, your attempts at that ultra-complicated money abundance spell may fall short. We call certain aspects of our practice basics, but they are far from it. They are a fundamental part of our craft and a foundation that can be added to and expanded upon for every year you are a witch. They aren't any less powerful, either. I have known practitioners who have spent five to ten years learning the "basics" and gotten so good at meditation and energetic work that they can cleanse a room with no materials. Speeding ahead to advanced magick is like trying to build a house on a shaky foundation: It may function, but it will not stand as strong as the house built on stone, and the longevity of the house might be questionable.

# THE MATERIALS
# OF SPELLCRAFT

From basic herbs and crystals to the tools of the witch, this chapter goes through each type of material, its associations, and uses. No materials in this chapter are considered necessary to complete the craft; they are merely what I have used and found helpful in mine and are elements you may wish to incorporate in yours.

The materials we use in witchcraft contain energy, as all living things do, and their properties stem from their uses and their folklore. When creating a spell, the goal is to match the intent of the materials to the intent of the spell. For example, if I was creating a spell to help me focus on my work, I would avoid herbs and crystals that have sedative or relaxing properties, like lavender or amethyst. Instead, I would choose to surround myself with crystals like sodalite—also known as the stone of teachers and writers—and use herbs in my spell like rosemary, which is said to improve memory; vanilla, which is said to strengthen mental abilities; and cloves, which it is said are helpful in clearing the mind.

I would use a colored candle that correlates with focus—green, blue, or, in magick, orange/yellow—and create a sigil, or a handmade symbol imbued with intent, to burn or keep in my studying area.

As explained in "The Basis of Spellcraft," materials are not always necessary. Sometimes the changes that need to be made can be achieved through active meditation, mindfulness, or an awareness of where we are putting our thoughts—even changing the way you think about yourself has the power to change your life. For more intermediate or advanced spells, such as those found later in this book, materials are sometimes necessary to push the outcome to where it needs to be. That's not to say you need fancy herbs or crystals for justice spells but a candle and some calendula (if you're winning a court case) may be of assistance. Part of the Craft is not simply using materials but using the materials that you have access to.

These materials are merely those that I have found of use most often in my practice, and those that I find most necessary to embark on the journey of manifesting change. All of the information about the materials, including correspondences and uses, has been sourced from the various books and encyclopedias which you can find at the back of this book. This list of spellcrafting materials has been carefully curated for you to use as a reference throughout your journey with the Craft, outlining the different tools, associations, and uses that will assist you within your practice.

# CRYSTALS

This section details different crystals, their elemental associations, and spiritual uses, as well as their chemical composition and physical properties like hardness (measured with the Mohs hardness scale). Depending on how hard the mineral is registered as, it may or may not be able to be submerged in water or placed with salt for cleansing. For example, a diamond is registered as a 10 on the Mohs scale, and gypsum (satin spar, selenite) is registered as a 2. A general rule of thumb is that softer crystals should be handled with more care and can break or dissolve easily in something like water. Anything softer than glass (hardness 5.5) shouldn't be submerged in water. However, like all rules, there are always exceptions, and these will be mentioned explicitly. It's important to note that some minerals and rocks sold as crystals can be hazardous to ingest. In general, even if something is considered "natural" this doesn't mean it is safe by default. Things like mercury and arsenic, which are naturally occurring, are known to be toxic to humans, just as certain plants can be. When a crystal is noted as toxic, please keep it out of the reach of animals and children and avoid ingesting.

Each of these crystals can be used to assist in specific spells by lending their energy or being charged to work within your everyday practice with particular intentions. Cleansing a crystal looks like clearing it of all the old energy that it could have collected, and this can be done through a variety of means:

1. Running it under water
2. Placing it in salt
3. Smoke cleansing
4. Placing it atop of selenite or a cleansing plate
5. Cleansing it in the moonlight

Charging the crystal means, quite simply, plugging your intent into the crystal in order for it to do its given job. This can look like meditating with the crystal, setting it on a paper written with intent, placing it in the sunlight, or even just beginning to work with the crystal again and again. If you employ the last method, you would typically have to use that specific crystal for one purpose. Before cleansing or charging your crystals, make sure they are not photosensitive and are not water soluble.

## QUARTZ

*All quartz is, in general, a stable and safe mineral to handle, and it is safe to submerge in water due to its hardness. This mineral is vitreous.*

### Clear quartz

**PROPERTIES:** Most common form of quartz, which as a mineral has a Mohs hardness rating of 7 and a vitreous or glasslike luster. In general, colors in quartz are due to inclusions or trace elements within the crystals.

**USES:** Easily charged with any intent, from protection to amplification, and is a fantastic stone to keep around for everyday use. Known as the master healer.

**FURTHER ASSOCIATIONS:** Cancer and Leo.

## Smoky quartz
**PROPERTIES:** A variant of quartz with a Mohs rating of 7. It is black and brown, and color can vary between being almost opaque to very transparent. The color is generally due to the trace element of aluminum within the crystal lattice.
**USES:** Smoky quartz is often noted as a crystal that can transmute negative energy into positive energy, thus being a go-to stone for empaths and highly sensitive people.
**FURTHER ASSOCIATIONS:** Capricorn, Sagittarius, and Scorpio, as well as the goddess Hekate.

## Rose quartz
**PROPERTIES:** A variant of quartz with a Mohs rating of 7. The color can be formed either through inclusion of the mineral dumortierite or through the inclusion of other trace elements in the crystal formation. Depending on how the color is formed within a particular stone, it can be vulnerable to fading with direct sunlight.
**USES:** Brings in love, healing, and compassion. Perfect for use in self-love spells or to carry with you on dates.
**FURTHER ASSOCIATIONS:** Deities of love, particularly Aphrodite. Also associated with Taurus and/or Libra.

## Amethyst
**PROPERTIES:** A variant of quartz with a Mohs rating of 7. The purple color of amethyst is due to the trace element of iron within the crystal lattice. The color is vulnerable to fading with direct sunlight.

**USES:** Amethyst is a healing stone said to have stress-relieving abilities that soothes anxiety, strain, and dissolves negativity.
**FURTHER ASSOCIATIONS:** Aquarius and the planet Jupiter. It is also February's birth stone.

### Citrine
**PROPERTIES:** A variety of quartz with a Mohs rating of 7. As with amethyst, the color of citrine often comes from the trace element of iron. Citrine also changes color at higher temperatures, and is vulnerable to fading with direct sunlight. Amethyst, being more common than citrine, is often heat-treated to produce similar colors, then sold as citrine.
**USES:** Citrine is considered a stone that is completely unaffected by negative energy, therefore it never needs to be cleansed. It can be used to draw in confidence, focus, and abundance, and is nicknamed "the success stone."
**FURTHER ASSOCIATIONS:** Virgo and Sagittarius, and the god Mercury.

### Aventurine
**PROPERTIES:** A variety of microcrystalline quartz with a Mohs rating of 6.5 to 7. Contains glistening fragments of mica and sometimes fuchsite or hematite. It is often green but can also be shades of brown, blue, and sometimes peach.
**USES:** Aventurine is a stone of healing and can be used for this purpose over the mind, body, and spirit.
**FURTHER ASSOCIATIONS:** Libra and Taurus, and the element of air with no known deity associations.

### Tiger's eye

**PROPERTIES:** A variety of quartz with a Mohs rating of 7. Tiger's eye has distinctive colors and visual texture. Although Tiger's eye is usually seen as a variety of quartz, it is often made up of more than one mineral.

**USES:** Tiger's eye is known to be a fantastic crystal for grounding and contains an earthy energy. It can be used to assist in gaining courage and confidence, as well as insight in certain situations, and issues of personal power.

**FURTHER ASSOCIATIONS:** Leo and Capricorn, as well as the planet earth and the sun.

## CHALCEDONY

*A common name and can refer to two different types. In this section I am using the definition that refers to microcrystalline quartz in general. All varieties of chalcedony will therefore also have a hardness of 7 on the Mohs scale, and not react or dissolve in water unless noted.*

### Agate

**PROPERTIES:** "Agate" is a term used to describe any chalcedony that is translucent. Agates are primarily found within volcanic and metamorphic rocks, and include a variety of colors with different associations, such as green, purple, grey, moss, tree, and fire.

**USES:** Agate is generally used as a stabilizing crystal. Blue lace agate is known as a great nurturing stone that helps with communicative abilities. Moss and tree agate, like their namesakes, are grounding and stabilizing stones. Fire agate is a protective stone, said to build a defensive shield around the body.

FURTHER ASSOCIATIONS: Different agates have different Zodiac and deity associations, including Gemini, Taurus, Virgo, and Capricorn.

## Carnelian

PROPERTIES: A reddish-brown to blood-red variety of chalcedony with a vitreous wax-like luster.

USES: Carnelian is said to inspire courage and raise confidence, and helps with public speaking. In ancient Egypt, Carnelian was used as a charm to ward off anger, jealousy, and misfortune.

FURTHER ASSOCIATIONS: Leo and Taurus, and the goddess Isis.

## Jasper

PROPERTIES: Descriptive term for any type of chalcedony that is opaque. Because of the different physical structures, jasper can have a lower rating on the Mohs scale, between 6.5 and 7.

USES: Red and tiger jasper are highly protective stones, known to promote organization. Ocean jasper is used to promote healing and peace. Yellow jasper is used as a stress reliever and leopardskin jasper is heavily associated with self-healing. Jasper is said to ward against trickster spirits.

FURTHER ASSOCIATIONS: All jasper is associated with Venus and/or Mars.

## Onyx

PROPERTIES: A variety of agate that is either black- or white-banded, sometimes monochromatic. Like jasper, different physical structures can give this crystal a lower rating on the Mohs scale, ranging between 6.5 and 7. Sardonyx is a variety of onyx with red and white bands.

**USES:** Many onyx stones are used to help increase focus, discipline, and recovery from stress. Onyx is often used for grounding and centering because of its strong ties to the earth.

**FURTHER ASSOCIATIONS:** Capricorn.

## Bloodstone

**PROPERTIES:** A variety of prase (dark green chalcedony or jasper) with blood-red spots, hence the name. Also known as heliotrope. Due to its structure, it ranks lower on the Mohs scale, at a 6.

**USES:** Bloodstone is said to increase immunity and clean the blood, as well as draw in wealth, clam fear and anger, and ensure success in legal matters.

**FURTHER ASSOCIATIONS:** Aries, Pisces, and Scorpio, and the planet/god Mars.

## FELDSPAR

*The most common mineral in the earth's crust with only a few crystal or gem-quality varieties. Feldspars are a group of minerals that can have a variable amount of potassium, sodium, and calcium. They are generally split into two groups: the alkali feldspars and the plagioclase feldspars. They are generally safe and stable and non-water soluble.*

## Labradorite

**PROPERTIES:** A plagioclase feldspar with a Mohs rating of 6 to 6.5. The shimmer it holds can be known as labradorescence.

**USES:** Many qualities are attributed to labradorite, including protection, enhanced psychic powers, banishing negative energies, good luck, and help with lucid dreaming. It assists in helping a practitioner with their intuition and dealing with the subconscious.

**FURTHER ASSOCIATIONS:** Aquarius, Leo, Sagittarius, and Scorpio, as well as the deities Isis and Arianrhod.

### Amazonite

**PROPERTIES:** A microcline alkali feldspar with a Mohs rating of 6 to 6.5. It is also known as Amazonstone and can be bright green/blue and white due to inclusions of lead or sometimes iron. Amazonite is photosensitive, and sometimes sunlight can actually enrich the colors of the brilliant stone.

**USES:** Said to help someone with balancing, love, and harmony, as well as bringing courage and luck to whoever carries it.

**FURTHER ASSOCIATIONS:** Virgo.

### Moonstone

**PROPERTIES:** An alkali feldspar known for its pearly and opalescent appearance.

**USES:** Said to help with intuition and accepting cyclical changes, as well as destiny. Moonstone is heavily associated with the full moon, and is a great stone to assist in any full moon workings.

**FURTHER ASSOCIATIONS:** Gemini and the moon, lunar deities.

## TOURMALINE

*Tourmaline is a crystal compounded with many different elements, including but not limited to aluminum, iron, magnesium, sodium, lithium, or potassium. It comes in a variety of colors including black, green, and even blue.*

### Black tourmaline

**PROPERTIES:** A crystal that's part of the aluminum borosilicate family that includes magnesium, iron, and other metals. Black tourmaline is a 7 to 7.5 on the Mohs hardness scale.

**USES:** Black tourmaline is a highly protective stone used to ward off negative energy. Keep it on windowsills or under your pillows to assist in keeping away nightmares.

**FURTHER ASSOCIATIONS:** The planet Pluto, therefore the Roman god Pluto and his Grecian counterpart, Hades, and the astrological sign Scorpio. Its elemental ruler is earth.

## GYPSUM

*Known as evaporite deposits. The gypsums in this section are soluble, but some varieties are food-safe. Do not, under any circumstances, breathe in the dust from gypsum, and if you do plan on consuming gypsum, please ensure the type you are using is food-safe.*

### Selenite

**PROPERTIES:** "Selenite" is a general gem name for a variety of the mineral gypsum, historically used to describe the transparent variety. Selenite has a Mohs rating of 2.

**USES:** Selenite is often touted as an intense cleansing crystal and can be used to cleanse the crystals around it. Selenite can be used to activate your other crystals as well as dispel negative energies.

**FURTHER ASSOCIATIONS:** The name is derived from Selene, Hellenic goddess of the moon, therefore it has associations with the moon and the element of water. It is also associated with Taurus.

### Desert rose

**PROPERTIES:** A rose-like crystal group formed mostly in arid desert regions and containing trapped sand particles. Desert rose has a Mohs rating of 2 and is named for the shape it grows into, rather than any difference in composition.

**USES:** Desert rose, similar to selenite, is a powerful cleansing crystal. It allows room for intuitive work, mental clarity, purification, and prosperity.

**FURTHER ASSOCIATIONS:** Scorpio, Capricorn, and Taurus.

### Satin spar

**PROPERTIES:** A fibrous variety of gypsum with a Mohs rating of 2. Satin spar is often sold as selenite, but it is fibrous while selenite tends to be smoother. Satin spar is, like desert rose, named for its appearance, not because there is a difference in composition.

**USES:** Satin spar has similar qualities to selenite, much like desert rose, including its cleansing properties.

**FURTHER ASSOCIATIONS:** Taurus.

## MICA
*Widely used in cosmetics to add the "sparkle/shimmer" that you will often see in products like eyeshadows and highlighters.*

### Lepidolite
**PROPERTIES:** A type of crystal, pink to purple in color. Lepidolite is a 2.5 to 3.5 on the Mohs scale. Lepidolite contains a high amount of the chemical lithium and so consumption of this crystal, or placing portions of it in any elixirs, formulas, or other items prepared for consumption, is not recommended. As well as this, be careful of the dust from lepidolite. Since it is a mica, it can break easily due to its softness.
**USES:** Lepidolite is known as a "stone of transition," aiding in change and allowing the practitioner to let go of restrictive beliefs and thought patterns. Lepidolite is used to dispel negativity and brings about deep emotional healing.
**FURTHER ASSOCIATIONS:** Libra.

## OTHER RECOMMENDED CRYSTALS
*The below are crystals that do not fall within the above families that can also be used within your practice.*

### Kyanite
**PROPERTIES:** With a Mohs rating of 5.5 to 7, there are different varieties of kyanite, including black kyanite, which often appears in fans, and blue kyanite. Some say that the sword of Archangel Michael was made of kyanite, making it able to cut through any mistruth.

**USES:** Kyanite is said to help dispel nightmares, protect against negativity, and increase psychic powers. It is also extremely useful in truth and justice workings.

**FURTHER ASSOCIATIONS:** Kyanite is associated with multiple Zodiac signs, including Aries, Libra, Taurus, and Pisces.

### Hematite

**PROPERTIES:** An iron oxide belonging to the hematite group with a 5 to 6 on the Mohs scale. Hematite can be a variety of colors, including reddish-brown, dark and silvery-gray, as well as black crystals. All hematite has a rust-red streak. Do not ingest this crystal.

**USES:** Sometimes known as a calming crystal, or a crystal of the mind, it is useful in grounding and protection for empaths. Hematite is a protective stone and is sometimes cited as a stone for self-healing.

**FURTHER ASSOCIATIONS:** Aries and Aquarius, as well as the planet Mars.

### Fluorite

**PROPERTIES:** A member of the fluorite group with a Mohs rating of 3.175 to 3.56. Fluorite comes in different colors, including clear, green, and purple, and sometimes a mix. It is a corrosive mineral and will fade in the sun, so please take proper precautions if you are shaping or grinding down fluorite, and do not leave in sunlight. Do not ingest this crystal.

**USES:** Fluorite is said to balance out emotions and neutralize negativity and stress. It is used to encourage confidence and positivity.

**FURTHER ASSOCIATIONS:** Capricorn and Pisces.

## Malachite

**PROPERTIES:** A green-colored and common mineral with a Mohs rating of 3.5 to 4. Malachite contains a large amount of copper, therefore should not be submerged in water or ingested. When the crystal is placed in water, it will become toxic.

**USES:** Malachite is known as a stone that will remove anything you do not need from your life. It is said to warn of impending danger by breaking. Malachite is known as the "salesperson's stone," so in folklore it is kept in or near a place of business to bring in prosperity for that person.

**FURTHER ASSOCIATIONS:** Scorpio, and the deities Venus and Freyja.

## Sodalite

**PROPERTIES:** A crystal that comes in a variety of colors, with a Mohs rating of 5.5 to 6.

**USES:** Sodalite is well-known for helping with focus, often touted as the stone of teachers. It can be used to bring forth truthfulness and logic in difficult situations.

**FURTHER ASSOCIATIONS:** Cancer.

## ROCKS

*There are three main groupings for rocks based on how they are formed: igneous (from melt), sedimentary (from eroded sediment), and metamorphic (igneous or sedimentary rocks that have been exposed to high pressures and/or temperatures).*

### Obsidian

**PROPERTIES:** A glassy and igneous rock with a high silica content. Rather than being a mineral, obsidian is a volcanic glass, meaning it cooled so quickly that no crystals were able to form. It's possible to think of this substance as frozen magma/lava. Obsidian has a Mohs rating of 5 to 6.

**USES:** Obsidian is a highly protective stone known to guard against and dispel all negativity. It can be used to help clear unconscious blocks when meditated with, and is said to be fantastic at grounding and healing unconscious wounds. It is said that obsidian will help someone see their flaws and change accordingly.

**FURTHER ASSOCIATIONS:** Sagittarius, Scorpio, and Aries. Obsidian also has associations with the Egyptian god Sekhmet.

### Lapis lazuli

**PROPERTIES:** An uncommon metamorphic rock having lazurite as its most common component along with other minerals like calcite, sodalite, and pyrite. It is a 5 to 5.5 on the Mohs scale.

**USES:** Lapis lazuli can be used to attract love and heighten intuition and psychic powers, as well as helping the practitioner to separate the conscious and subconscious mind.

**FURTHER ASSOCIATIONS:** It has associations to wisdom, knowledge, perfection, creative expression, and protection. Lapis lazuli is associated with the signs Sagittarius and Capricorn, as well as the deities Nuit, Venus, and Isis.

### Jet

**PROPERTIES:** A hard, gem-quality hydrocarbon. The term "jet" is given to many materials across the world with similar properties, but most have been framed through different processes. It forms in a similar—but not exactly the same—way to coal when pieces are buried in sediment. Its Mohs rating is between 2.5 and 4.

**USES:** Jet is a protective stone, often used to keep negative entities and energies away. It's fantastic for empaths due to the protection it is said to give against energetic vampires, and it can be used to guard against nightmares.

**FURTHER ASSOCIATIONS:** Capricorn, and deities Pan and Cybele.

# HERBS

*Herbs are used for a variety of reasons within the Craft, including, but not limited to, being added to spells, burned, or used as their own charms within the witch's practice. Herbs hold innate magickal properties that can be called upon, and this list does not include all the herbs used in witchcraft, but rather the ones I am most familiar with and use most to create a foundational starting point for beginners. I have tried to focus the attention on herbs that you may have in your kitchen or are accessible to the average buyer. The associations I have listed are based on origin and folklore, and their uses can easily be correlated and referenced again and again for use in your own spell work.*

### Oregano (*Origanum vulgare*)
USES: Oregano is a common cooking herb that can be used to bring in money, love, joy, and health, or to add overall satisfaction to the spell results. I like to use oregano in my cooking to bring in health and joy to the household, or you can place in money spells to bring in prosperity.
FURTHER ASSOCIATIONS: Ruled by Venus and associated with the element of air.

### Feverfew (*Chrysanthemum parthenium*)
USES: Feverfew is used for protection. When carried with you, folklore says it can protect from colds and fevers, and accidents.
FURTHER ASSOCIATIONS: The planet Venus and the element of water.

### Thyme (*Thymus vulgaris*)

USES: Thyme is used for health and healing, sleep, courage, psychic powers, and purification. The folklore of thyme says that wearing it or burning it will bring about good health, courage, and energy. The ancient Greeks burned thyme in their temples as a purification. I tend to use thyme in my protective charm bags.

FURTHER ASSOCIATIONS: Venus and water.

### Mint (different varieties of the genus *Mentha*)

USES: Mint is used for money, protection, communication, healing, travel, lust, and exorcism. In Greek mythos, Minthe was a naiad who was loved by Hades. When she declared herself above Hades' wife, Persephone, the goddess turned her into a mint plant. Thus, the mint plant has associations with the Grecian god of the underworld. Folklore states that mint can be used to provoke lust and help with travel, and placing a few leaves in the wallet will bring in prosperity. Keeping mint in the home helps with protection.

FURTHER ASSOCIATIONS: Mercury and the element air.

### Fennel (*Foeniculum vulgare*)

USES: Fennel is used for protection, healing, purification, strength, and sexual virility. Folklore states that fennel, grown around the home, protects the hearth. It can be hung up in windows and doors to ward off evil spirits or carried for the same reason. I use fennel in my positivity spells or witch bottles (see pages 157, 112–13)

FURTHER ASSOCIATIONS: The planet Mercury and the element of fire.

### Aniseed (*Pimpinella anisum*)

USES: Aniseed is used for protection, purification, helping with psychic power, and bringing changes in attitude. Folklore says that dreaming on aniseed in a satchel will ensure that you have good dreams and aniseed leaves placed in a room will drive away evil. Aniseed is said to avert the evil eye and can call forth spirits. I tend to use it in my domination magick and protective satchels.

FURTHER ASSOCIATIONS: Aniseed is ruled by the planet Jupiter and the element of air.

### Mugwort (*Artemisia vulgaris*)

USES: Mugwort is a powerful herb used in strengthening psychic powers, protection, prophetic dreams, healing, and astral projection. Folklore states that when carrying mugwort you cannot be harmed by poison, wild beasts, or sunstroke. Mugwort can be used to increase lust and fertility by carrying, and placing it next to the bed aids in astral projection. I use mugwort in most of my protective spells.

FURTHER ASSOCIATIONS: Mugwort is associated with the moon as it is sacred to Artemis and Diana, as well as Venus and the element of earth.

SAFETY NOTE: Many practitioners have taken to consuming mugwort, so it must be stated that mugwort is a known abortive—please do not handle or consume mugwort if you are pregnant or trying to get pregnant, and *always* speak to a medical professional before consuming herbs.

### Rue (*Ruta graveolens*)

**USES:** Rue is used for protection (especially against the evil eye), healing, health, love, and freedom. Rue is a fantastic banishing herb, and can be burned to remove unpleasant or unwanted spirits from the space. Adding rue to a bath will banish any negativity or harmful magick placed upon you. I use rue in a herb bundle to cleanse my altar space, keep my house protected, and cast circles for spell work alongside rosemary.

**FURTHER ASSOCIATIONS:** The planet Mars and the element of fire.

**SAFETY NOTE:** Like mugwort, rue is a known abortive. Please do not handle or consume if you are pregnant or trying to get pregnant.

### Bay leaves (*Laurus nobilis*)

**USES:** Bay leaves are used for protection, psychic powers, healing, purification, and strength. Apollo's priestesses in ancient Greece chewed bay leaves to induce a prophetic state and inhaled their fumes. An age-old ritual is writing a wish on a bay leaf and burning it to bring it into existence. I like to use bay leaves to cleanse, as well as writing intentions on them as part of my spell work.

**FURTHER ASSOCIATIONS:** The sun, as a sacred herb of Apollo, as well as the element of fire.

### Morning glory (different variations under the genus *Ipomoea*, also known as bindweed)

**USES:** Morning glory is extremely useful in binding spells, banishments, and promoting attraction. I use morning glory vines frequently in binding spells, either binding with the vine itself or including them within the paper if I use thread to bind.

FURTHER ASSOCIATIONS: The planet Saturn and the element of water.
SAFETY NOTE: Morning glory is poisonous. Make sure you wash
your hands before and after handling and do not, under any
circumstances, consume.

### Elder (*Sambucus canadensis*)
USES: Elder is used for spells around exorcism, protection, healing,
prosperity, and sleep. Elderflowers are very useful in sleep satchels,
and wearing them is said to ward off evil and attackers. The
flowers hung over doorways are used to keep evil away.
FURTHER ASSOCIATIONS: Venus and the element of water.
SAFETY NOTE: Raw elderberries, leaves, roots, and bark are
poisonous. Use with caution.

### Vervain (*Verbena officinalis*)
USES: Vervain is used for love, protection, purification, peace, money,
youth, sleep, and healing. In ancient Rome, priests used vervain to
clean the altars of Jupiter. Keep vervain in the home or bury in the
yard to bring in wealth, protect from storms, and bring peace.
FURTHER ASSOCIATIONS: Vervain is a powerful protective herb
and sacred to multiple deities, including Cerridwen, Mars, Venus,
Aradia, Isis, Jupiter, Thor, and Juno. It is associated with the planet
Venus and the element of earth.
SAFETY NOTE: Vervain, although found in many supplements and
touted as a popular remedy, is only safe at the recommended
medical doses. Potential toxicity can occur with misuse of the herb,
so please only ingest vervain at the behest of medical professionals
and at the approved dosage.

### Cinnamon (*Cinnamomum zeylanicum*)

USES: Cinnamon is used for spirituality, healing, power, protection, love, luck, and prosperity. Throughout history, cinnamon has been used for different purposes—in ancient Rome, it was added to anointing oils as it was believed to enhance libido as well as being a source of sexual strength. In ancient Egypt, cinnamon oil was used in the mummification process as a perfuming and embalming agent. Cinnamon can be burned as incense to enhance psychic powers, or added to protective satchels. Cinnamon can also be used in money spells to bring in prosperity.

FURTHER ASSOCIATIONS: The sun and fire.

### Cloves (*Syzygium aromaticum* or *Caryophyllus aromaticus*)

USES: Cloves are used for protection, exorcism, love, and money. Folklore says that wearing cloves brings forth protection and mental clarity, and burning cloves as incense is said to stop gossip and purify the area, driving away any unhelpful forces. I frequently use cloves to "heat up" a spell, adding protection and an element of quickness to my magick.

FURTHER ASSOCIATIONS: The planet Jupiter and the element of fire.

### Yarrow (*Achillea millefolium*)

USES: Yarrow is used for courage, love, healing, and divination. Yarrow flowers are known to draw in love and are said to keep a newly married couple happy for seven years. Because of this, yarrow can be used in self-love satchels and healing spells, or just be kept around the home to bring in positivity.

FURTHER ASSOCIATIONS: The planet Venus and the element of water.

### Valerian root (*Valeriana officinalis*)

USES: Valerian root is used in purification, love, sleep, dreams, harmony, and protection. Valerian root can be used for several purposes, including adding it to protective satchels, hanging it in windows to ward off evil, or putting it under your pillow to aid in sleep. Some say wearing it will calm the emotions, and burning it can reconcile relationships. I like to add valerian to my purification and protection spells.

FURTHER ASSOCIATIONS: Venus and the element of water.

### Rosemary (*Rosmarinus officinalis*)

USES: Rosemary is used for protection, love, lust, healing, purification, and removal of negativity. Carrying rosemary is said to assist in clearing your head and it is a powerful protector that can be used in smoke cleansing. Rosemary is a known substitute for frankincense, and can also be used in healing or love spells. One of my staple herbs, I keep an herb bundle of it on my ancestral altar, and the dried herb by itself for a particular protection jar.

FURTHER ASSOCIATIONS: The sun and the element of fire.

## Basil (*Ocimum basilicum*)

USES: Basil is used for wealth, protection, and love. Basil is known to drive off fear and hostile spirits, and is heavily associated with the Catholic holiday Candlemas. It is said that where basil lives, no evil can—so it can be strewn upon floors, carried with you, or kept as a plant in the house for protection. Carrying basil is also said to bring in prosperity. Add basil to your money spells in the form of a satchel to attract success and keep a basil plant by your door to stave off malevolent spirits.

FURTHER ASSOCIATIONS: The planet Mars and the element of fire.

## Wormwood (*Artemisia absinthium*)

USES: Wormwood is used for protection, psychic powers, love, calling spirits, and warding off the evil eye. It can be burned as an incense to heighten psychic powers or call in spirits. Wormwood is an herb that can often be substituted for mugwort, and vice versa.

FURTHER ASSOCIATIONS: The planet Mars and the element of fire.

SAFETY NOTE: Commonly known for its use in absinthe, this plant can be toxic and/or fatal in large amounts, so please do not consume.

## Garden sage (*Salvia officinalis*)

USES: Garden sage is used for wisdom, longevity, protection, wishes, and self-purification. Garden sage is a well-known substitute for the threatened white sage (*S. apiana*) and can be used for smoke cleansing, spiritual and mental health, and longevity. It is said that if you write a wish on a sage leaf, leave it under your pillow for three nights, and dream of the wish, it will come true—if the wish does not appear in your dreams, you have to bury the sage leaf to ensure no harm will come to you. Sage can be used in protective satchels, as a purifying incense, or sometimes to guard against the evil eye.

**FURTHER ASSOCIATIONS:** The planet Jupiter and the element of air.

# FURTHER NATURAL MATERIALS

*Other materials from nature such as flowers, trees, vegetables, and kitchen materials.*

## FLOWERS AND FLOWERING PLANTS

### Hibiscus (variety of herbs in the genus *Hibiscus*)

USES: Hibiscus is used for lust and love. Burn hibiscus to bring in love, or carry in a satchel for the same effect. Use it in your self-love spells, or do tea magick with hibiscus.

FURTHER ASSOCIATIONS: Venus and the element of water.

### Jasmine (*Jasminum officinale* or *J. odoratissimum*)

USES: Jasmine is used for purification, wisdom, and prophetic dreams. It is fantastic for charging crystals. To do so, place crystals in a bag with jasmine flowers. Jasmine can also be used in protective or purification spells and sleep satchels, a small bag or packet for various uses, to promote good dreams.

FURTHER ASSOCIATIONS: The moon and the element of water.

### Rose (different varieties under the genus *Rosa*)

USES: Rose is used for love divination, psychic powers, healing, luck, and protection. Roses and rose petals can be used in protective or self-love spells, and rose thorns can be used for particular protection spells or within baneful magick.

FURTHER ASSOCIATIONS: Venus and the element of water.

### Geranium (different varieties under the genus *Pelargonium*)

USES: Geranium is said to avert negativity and gossip. Geranium root can be carried with you to attract prosperity, and it can be used in fertility spells to encourage successful conception and a safe childbirth.

FURTHER ASSOCIATIONS: Venus and Mercury and the element of water.

### Primrose (different varieties under the genuses *Primulacae* and *Oenothera*)

USES: Primrose can be used to uncover secrets and bring about a revelation of truth, and is extremely powerful in truth spells. Evening primrose is tied to the goddess Diana, and can be used in beauty rituals and moon ceremonies.

FURTHER ASSOCIATIONS: The Moon.

### Hydrangea (*Hydrangea arborescens*)

USES: Hydrangea is used for hex breaking, bindings, and fidelity. The bark of hydrangea is a well-known hex-breaker, and can be used in return to sender (see page 137) or uncrossing spells, which are specific spells used to remove obstacles, road blocks, or "crosses" that have been placed upon you. Hydrangea, when planted on your property, is said to bring protection and boundaries. My family has hydrangea plants lining the front of our yard.

FURTHER ASSOCIATIONS: The moon, Jupiter, and Neptune, and the element of water.

### Chamomile (*Anthemis nobilis*)

**USES:** Chamomile is used for money, purification, love, sleep, and reducing stress. Adding chamomile to a spell increases its success and the herb is often used to attract money. It is said that sprinkling chamomile around your house will remove any baneful magick placed upon you. Chamomile is also used to attract love. Drink chamomile tea before bed to assist with sleep and relaxation, or add the herb to your protective wards to keep away harmful magick.

**FURTHER ASSOCIATIONS:** The sun and the element of water.

### Lavender (*Lavandula officinalis*)

**USES:** Lavender is used for love, sleeping, protection, healing, and peace. Lavender can be used in any spell to bring in relaxation, including lavender tea magick before bed. In folklore, lavender can also be carried for seeing ghosts and protection against the evil eye. For this reason, I tend to use lavender in my protective charms and drink lavender tea before communing with the divine.

**FURTHER ASSOCIATIONS:** Mercury, and the element of air.

### Marigold/Calendula (*Calendula officinalis*)

**USES:** Marigold is used for justice, protection, legal matters, prophetic dreams, and psychic powers. In folklore, marigolds strung into garlands and hung in front of the house will stop evil entering the home, and placed below your bed it will protect you in your sleep. For this reason, I tend to include calendula flowers in most of my protective sleep satchels.

**FURTHER ASSOCIATIONS:** The sun and the element of fire.

## TREES

### Cedar (*Cedrus* and *Thuja*)

**USES:** Cedar is used for healing, purification, money, confidence, and protection. Cedar is a genus of coniferous trees in the plant family Pinaceae found all over the world, including *C. libani*, or Lebanese cedar. The western red cedar, *T. plicata*, actually belongs to a different genus in the Cupressaceae family. The varieties of cedar are, for the most part, in stable populations and currently not of concern to conservationists and environmental groups. Cedar leaf bundles for smoke cleansing are a popular substitute for white sage, and it's said that cedar kept in the wallet or purse draws in prosperity. Hanging cedar in the hearth is said to protect against lightning. A common substitute is juniper.

**FURTHER ASSOCIATIONS:** The sun and the element of fire.

### Juniper (*Juniperus communis*)

**USES:** Juniper is used as a powerful banishing herb as well as for protection, love, and health. It is said that juniper hung on the door protects against evil forces and theft, and juniper berries, when carried by men, can increase potency. I use juniper berries in offerings to a patron deity, Cernunnos.

**FURTHER ASSOCIATIONS:** The sun and the element of fire.

### Birch (*Betula alba*)

**USES:** Birch is used in protection and purification. Birch near the home is known to ward off and protect against the evil eye, as well as lightning. My family has three birch trees planted beside the home, albeit not for magickal purposes, and the bark can be used in protective spells.

**FURTHER ASSOCIATIONS:** Venus and the element of water.

## VEGETABLES

### Garlic (*Allium sativum*)

**USES:** Garlic is used for protection, healing, exorcism, and anti-theft. While garlic is often associated with the goddess Hekate and sometimes, because of this, the moon, another association is Archangel Michael. Garlic is said to contain the essence of Archangel Michael and, because of this, folk practitioners in Italy and Italian immigrants in America hung garlands of garlic in their home for protection. Garlic can be used in protective charms and satchels and is a common staple in kitchen witchery. You can add garlic cloves to your bath to banish negativity, or carry a clove with you to achieve the same goal.

**FURTHER ASSOCIATIONS:** The planet Mars and the element of fire.

### Chili peppers (different plants under the genus *Capsicum*)

**USES:** Chili peppers are used for fidelity, hexing, love, and hex breaking. The various types of chili pepper have different properties. For example, cayenne (*C. annuum*) is used in repelling negativity and speeding up any spell it is added to. Bird's eye chilis from the Solanaceae (nightshade) family can be used for cursing and crafting powders. Chili peppers and powders are generally used in both sowing discord and bane in the lives of targets, but also to break hexes by scattering the powder around the house. Chili powder has also been used in love charms and spells to increase attraction.

**FURTHER ASSOCIATIONS:** The planet Mars and the element of fire.

### Onion (*Allium cepa*)

**USES:** Onion is used for protection, exorcism, healing, prophetic dreams, and endurance. Folklore states that you can take a small white onion, fill it with black-headed pins by sticking them all over, and place it in a window to protect the home from evil. Halved or quartered and placed in the home, onions will absorb negativity and diseases before you then bury them in the morning.

**FURTHER ASSOCIATIONS:** Mars and the element of fire.

### Potato (*Solanum tuberosum*)

**USES:** Potatoes are used for image magic and healing spells. Potatoes, similar to onions, can be used as poppets in sympathetic and image magic by writing the name of the target on the potato or placing the name of the target in the potato.

**FURTHER ASSOCIATIONS:** The moon and the earth.

## KITCHEN MATERIALS

### Eggshells

**USES:** Eggshells are used for protection. Eggshells can be ground up into a powder and placed around the house for protection. They are often quoted as keeping non-corporeal or unfriendly entities away and can be used in various protection spells. Unlike salt, spreading eggshells around your home won't damage the earth and the plants inhabiting it, and they are a great fertilizer.

**FURTHER ASSOCIATIONS:** Eggshells are sometimes associated with the moon due to its associations with fertility.

### Salt

**USES:** By far the most used purification tool, salt of all forms is a well-known cleansing device. Sea salt in its different forms is used for cleansing crystals, protection magick, and purification. Salt is associated with the element earth, and can be used for casting circles. Black salt can be used to absorb negativity, so when this type is used, it's important to switch out the salt with new black salt to refresh it every so often. When used outside, on earth, salt can damage the soil and surrounding plants, so creating outdoor wards is a job better done with eggshells. Salt placed on windowsills can keep negative entities at bay, and salt used in protective charms has a purifying effect. Throw salt into four corners of the room and sweep up to cleanse, or use it in your floor washes to get the same effect (make sure you check that saltwater will not damage your floors!). Salt can also be used in cleansing bowls to soak up negative energy and purify a space, and a saltwater spray can be created to spritz on doorways and windows of the house for cleansing.

Another way to use salt for warding—a form of protective magick—is to draw protective sigils (see pages 70–75) with saltwater on your doors and/or windows.

**FURTHER ASSOCIATIONS:** Multiple planets including earth.

### Lemon (*Citrus limon*)

**USES:** Lemon is used for purification, hexing, and cleansing. Often the juice of a lemon is sourced as a purification tool that can be used in many rituals, including in purifying mixes and washes for floors, amulets, windowsills, etc. Place lemon slices covered in salt around your house to absorb negative energy—if the lemons molder, they must be disposed of and redone, but if they dry up and shrink, they have successfully removed the negativity. You can add lemon slices or juice to uncrossing and purification baths. Lemons, for their bitter qualities, can also be used to sour a target's life, or be used as poppets. Placing a target's name inside a lemon, or using lemon juice, rind, or slices in hexes and curses can effectively make your target's life bitter.

**FURTHER ASSOCIATIONS:** The moon and the element of water.

## WATER

*Water is used to quench the thirst of spirits and divine beings, as well as being able to be charged with different celestial energies (sun and moon). Different waters hold different properties. I've listed a few and their uses on the following page:*

## Moon water

**PROPERTIES:** Water charged under the light of the moon.
The properties of the water change depending on the moon cycle
the water is charged in. For example, full moon water would be
protective and cleansing, but new moon water could assist in
banishment works.

## Sun water

**PROPERTIES:** Water charged under the sun, often touted as having
properties of bringing joy and happiness into a spell.

## Storm water

**PROPERTIES:** Water collected from different types of storms, which
will have different properties depending on the storm you collect it
from. Rainwater or water collected during a "calm" storm can help
with calming, but water collected during more intense storms, like
hurricanes and thunderstorms, can be used to add power to a spell.

## Blessed water

**PROPERTIES:** Blessed water is simply that—water that has been
blessed. This can also be replaced with holy water, blessing it
yourself with certain prayers (pagan or otherwise) that you are
comfortable with, such as the Hail Mary, a specific number of
times that is considered lucky or blessed (three, nine, sixteen,
thirteen, depending on the folklore).

# TOOLS

*A witch's tools can be used for crafting spells, divination, and adding accuracy and efficiency to their practice. All tools in this area are optional, but are merely what I use in my craft and are fully adaptable to yours.*

## SCISSORS

Although some practitioners opt for an athame—a ceremonial and sacred knife—I tend to prefer scissors. I consider them safer, and much easier to use to cut cords, papers, and more while retaining the ability to gesture and point at things, like the athame. I also find that scissors are often more readily available and easier to access.

## BOOK OF SHADOWS

The book of shadows is considered almost like a personal spell book. It can contain information valuable to your practice, notes, rituals, and overall it helps you keep track of your craft's tools, spells, etc. Grimoire is often used interchangeably with the term "book of shadows," but a grimoire will usually be less personal, like information to pass down through the family. Whether you keep a book of shadows is completely up to you—I have known witches who choose only to write down certain aspects of spell work, witches who work completely intuitively, and witches who record everything. Contrary to popular belief, your book of shadows doesn't have to be in a big leather book with a pretty symbol on the front. My book of shadows is a 93-page Word document, where I can easily add and change aspects of my written craft, including updating rituals and information as they change. I knew a practitioner who kept their book of shadows in a binder, easily adding and removing pages as they pleased. A nice leather notebook is definitely aesthetically pleasing, but for someone who doesn't have access to many tools, a ringed notebook, binder, or even a notes page in your phone works fine.

## WAND

When we think of wands, we often picture the ones from *Harry Potter*. The real wands we use serve as a special way of directing energy, which is fantastic for those who have difficulty with this. They can also be used to cast a circle for spell casting. My first wand was a stick I felt especially drawn to that I rolled in herbs and consecrated by burning the edges slightly. I later made another wand that was carved and filed down, with three crystals attached at each end and the center. A wand doesn't necessarily have to be a fancy, wire-wrapped creation; it could be as plain as you like, and some witches even use *Harry Potter*–branded wands for their craft. Not all witches opt to use a wand, and that's perfectly fine.

## MORTAR AND PESTLE

This is by far one of my favorite tools to employ in the Craft. A mortar and pestle is used for grinding herbs together, crushing eggshells and the like. We often see this on herbalism sites, and though by no means necessary for the Craft, I have found it to be a valuable addition. Before my mortar and pestle, I used a bowl to mix herbs together by hand, which later became an offering bowl or a bowl to hold water as a spiritual gift.

## THE ALTAR

The witch's altar is a well-known tool with lots of variations ranging from seasonal altars, decorative altars, and working altars. I recommend Temperance Alden's *Year of the Witch* if you'd like to know more about them. A witch's altar can be considered a sacred space, where the practitioner does their workings and completes spell work, a space of devotion to certain spirits and entities, or a space to keep and charge items. Altars can be catered to different purposes, and different paths of witchcraft may have different altars. A Wiccan altar can be rather structured, whereas an eclectic witch's altar may seem a little more haphazard. When creating an altar, I recommend making it a space that feels magickal and sacred to you. Whether that means placing a few crystals and candles on a windowsill as a place to honor the universe, or just a place to hold items that you feel are sacred. For some inspiration, I have detailed the elements and purposes of my three altars on the following pages.

### Working/pagan altar

This altar is a place to worship my three pagan deity patrons, and includes a space for a candle and offerings for each of them. It also is a place for charging crystals, housing my wand, and keeping other tools. It also has a statue of Artemis, the Hellenic maiden goddess of the hunt; a plant; and some oils and herbal blends of my own making that I can employ in spell work when necessary.

### Saint and ancestor altar

My second altar is atop my supply cabinet, which holds my herbs, books, candles, mortar and pestle, and different materials that don't necessarily need to be charged consistently or are used less frequently. This altar space is primarily one of veneration, both of my ancestors and of my saints. My ancestors in this sense represent my hereditary family which stretches all the way back to hundreds of years ago. I honor them as well as my saints, sometimes referred to as spiritual ancestors, as part of my folk practice. The altar has a candle for Saint Mary, as well as a statue of her, blessed and cleansed; a candle for both my patron saint and Saint Michael the Archangel, as well as flash cards with each of their likenesses. It holds my first wand—a small, consecrated stick—my rosary beads, a book of novenas, offerings for each saint, a bowl for offerings for my ancestors, and a prayer plant that doubles as an offering and a ward. This altar is placed above my shoulder level to honor and venerate both my ancestors and my saints. While there are many different ways to create an ancestor altar, oftentimes a simple white candle and a glass of water will suffice.

## My desk

Surprisingly, I treat my desk as an altar. While my other altars hold some level of worship or offering for my spirits, my desk is purely a working altar. I keep long-term spells, like my box of manifestations, my spider plant, my aloe vera plant, and a few choice crystals (sodalite, selenite, blue lace agate) in this space. I use it primarily to write, which in turn is something I do that I consider sacred and part of my craft. I also heavily cleanse this space, and keep a few talismans and charms on it to inspire creativity in my work.

# DIVINATORY TOOLS

*Divinatory methods can be used to assist in seeking counsel for day-to-day problems or advice on a particular situation, or employed to talk to divine beings.*

## TAROT CARDS

The first Rider-Waite or Waite-Smith deck was published in 1909, illustrated by Pamela Colman Smith, an all-too-forgotten figure behind this famous tarot deck. The Waite-Smith and then Rider-Waite structure has become increasingly popular in occult and spiritual circles, and the original art has been incorporated into hundreds of different tarot decks—some stay true to the original symbolism but make the art more contemporary and inclusive, like the Modern Witch Tarot, and some more abstract, like the Mystic Monday Tarot.

Tarot has a set structure—the minor and major arcana: The minor arcana is defined by four suits—the wands, representing fire; the cups, representing water; the swords, representing air; and the pentacles, representing earth. Each suit has an ace through to a ten, aces representing new beginnings and unlimited potential, and the tens representing the end of a cycle, as well as four court cards—the page, the knight, the queen, and the king. The major arcana represents divine energy, or major life events, and runs from one, the Fool, to twenty-one, the World.

Modern-day tarot has several uses, one of which is to provide guidance on day-to-day issues. I often consult the cards daily to see what to focus on for the day or keep in the front of my mind. Some practitioners like to use tarot to help them with shadow work, and there are even specific decks, like the Dark Wood Tarot, that incorporate shadow work as a major theme in their art and guidebook. Tarot can be used to reflect on our own subconscious thoughts and intuition and is often used as a fantastic source to talk to divine beings when starting out. Tarot, at the end of the day, is still a tool, one which more often than not reflects your own intuition rather than giving way to hidden secrets from the universe. It helps us further understand our own psychic abilities and what we can feel and know from the divine, whether that's a deity, your higher self, or even just the universe in all its entirety.

I have used tarot cards for all of the above reasons, and often even structure my spells around them. For example, I use the Justice tarot card to help bring energy and focus to a spell whose end goal is to determine justice.

I often give tarot readings to friends and clients, and tend to be a strongly intuitive reader—meaning, when I pull a card, I tend to look at what the card means to me as well as the normal definition, while also considering what I am picking up on intuitively about the reading. Using spreads, or predetermined places for specific cards and their meanings, is a great way to start off working with your cards. There are tons of popular spreads, such as the Celtic Cross, a basic three-card spread detailing past, present, and future, and spreads to determine romantic situations. Some readers always use spreads and some always keep a book on hand with lists of the meanings for the cards. Whether you choose to read intuitively or prefer to keep the meanings on hand is up to you as the practitioner.

Even as a practitioner, you don't need to use tarot cards—some prefer other divinatory methods, like divination with bones, or divination using tea.

If you do choose to pursue tarot cards as a divinatory method, I've included a basic spread below.

**FIRST CARD:** The situation.

**SECOND CARD:** Your feelings about the situation.

**THIRD CARD:** Clarifier to ask why you feel that way about the situation.

**FOURTH CARD:** How you can work through the situation.

**FIFTH CARD:** How to move forward from the situation.

**SIXTH CARD:** What are you holding on to about the situation?

**SEVENTH CARD:** What do you need to let go of from the situation?

## PENDULUM

The pendulum is another divinatory method. A pendulum is usually demonstrated as a stone or crystal at the end of a chain, but, truthfully, a pendulum can be anything. My great-grandma used her wedding ring on the end of a string or a piece of hair, holding it over a pregnant woman's belly. Depending on whether the ring swayed clockwise or counterclockwise, she would know whether the woman would have a boy or a girl. I have known practitioners who tie a crystal to a string or piece of yarn and use it as a pendulum.

A pendulum is held either in the hand of the practitioner, or within a bottle, and a question is asked—usually a yes or no question. Sometimes you can write the alphabet out on a piece of paper, and ask for letter answers. There's some debate on how the pendulum works: if you're holding it in your hand, it could be responding to micro movements of muscles, another example of reflecting your intuition. Many practitioners prefer to create a pendulum bottle, a pendulum suspended within another object like a jar or bottle, where there is no room for micro movements of the hand to interfere.

Pendulums, as well as other divinatory devices, can be held in the hand of the practitioner and assist in the finding of lost things. For example, I happened to mislay a bracelet, so I held my pendulum in my hand, and asked for guidance on where it was. I watched the minute sways of the pendulum and followed them, stepping once in the direction the pendulum swayed and stopping to still my movements, then doing it again. I found my bracelet underneath my clothing dresser. I like choosing my pendulums in person and feeling whether I connect with them; or I use some of my well-loved rings on the end of red thread, similar to what my great-grandma did years ago.

## CANDLES

*Candles are used within magick to push the intent of the practitioner out into the universe. This works by using a particular color correspondence, size, and even oil and herb dressings to match with the spell. As the candle burns, the intent is sent up into the universe.*

## Color correspondences for candles

**WHITE:** protection, purification, truth, sincerity, peace, spirituality, workplace magick

**RED:** protection, strength, health, vigor, lust, sex, passion, courage

**BLACK:** absorbing/destroying negativity, healing, banishing, release, loss, rebirth

**BLUE:** tranquility, healing, patience, happiness, change, flexibility, subconscious, psychic powers, healing

**GREEN:** finances, fertility, luck, growth, creativity, prosperity

**GRAY:** neutrality

**YELLOW:** intellect, attraction, study, persuasion, success, confidence, divination, happiness

**BROWN:** working magick for animals, healing animals, spells for the home, material matters, grounding

**PINK:** love, humor, morality, friendship, beauty, fidelity, marriage

**ORANGE:** adaptability, stimulation, attraction, reconciliation, vitality

**SILVER:** healing, money, purification, psychic powers, fertility, divine receptive energy, stability

**PURPLE:** power, healing, spirituality, justice, mediation, authority, independence, wisdom

---

### Candle shape and size

This covers only a few of the candles I tend to use, but it goes to say that typically the bigger the candle, the longer the magick will be in effect.

**CHIME:** using a chime spell candle typically allows the spell to take effect for around a week

**TAPER:** using a taper candle typically allows the spell to take effect for around two to three weeks

**PILLAR/PRAYER:** pillar and prayer candles, depending on how big, can allow a spell to take hold for a month. Some of my prayer and pillar candles, which are made to burn for seven to nine days, I light a little bit every day, strengthening the spell.

---

## SIGILS

A sigil is less a tool and more a type of magick. A sigil is a particular type of symbol, often created by the practitioner themselves or by another practitioner on their behalf, that is often used in ritual magick. There are lots of popular sigils, like the sigil of Baphomet or the sigil of Lucifer, which can be found easily when researched.

Sigils were created from chaos magick, specifically by Austin Osman Spare. While some contacted spirit guides, Spare was creating particular symbols to manifest his specific desires. Sigil magick has since been more broadly adopted, but still remains a core part of the chaos magick approach. Specifically, Phil Hine in *Condensed Chaos* uses the acronym S.P.L.I.F.F. to explain sigil magick. It stands for:

**S**—Statement of intent
**P**—Pathways available?
**L**—Link intent to symbolic carrier
**I**—Intense gnosis/Indifferent vacuity
**F**—Fire
**F**—Forget

### Statement of intent

Sigils are created, first and foremost, with this. For example, if you are writing a spell, you could write out a petition or statement saying exactly what you want to come from the spell. If you are working with a money spell, you can write: "Money comes to me effortlessly and in abundance without depleting others."

### Pathways available?

This is about opening up a pathway for the sigil to take hold. What Hine means by this is the idea that your magick will work better if there is an open route available. Money may come easier to you if you are applying for a job, working on a new creative project you hope to sell and share, so on and so forth. You may have more trouble finding money and completing the spell, or notice the universe tends to manifest the money in an unexpected way, like a coworker being fired so your hours per week double. While not everyone may like Hine's approach to looking for pathways, it's still a great note to emphasize the importance of being specific in your magick.

### Link intent to symbolic carrier

Everyone has a specific way of doing this, but the way I prefer is this, that which Hine refers to as a monogram:

1. Write out your statement of intent.
2. Cross out all repeating letters. For example, if I write out:

### MONEY COMES TO ME EFFORTLESSLY AND IN ABUNDANCE WITHOUT DEPLETING OTHERS

It becomes:

### MONEY C~~OME~~S T~~O ME~~ EFF~~ORTLESSLY~~ AND I~~N~~ ~~A~~BU~~NDANCE~~ W~~ITH~~OU~~T~~ ~~DEPLETIN~~G ~~OTHERS~~

And then:

### MONEYCSTFRLADIBUWHPG

From here, I write out numbers one through nine, and then the alphabet below it, so it looks like this:

1 2 3 4 5 6 7 8 9
a b c d e f g h i
j k l m n o p q r
s t u v w x y z

I match up each letter I have left with the number that it is aligned with in the formation illustrated above, so M would be 4, O would be 6, N would be 5, so on and so forth, until I have this number combination:

**46557312693149235877**

Looks like a bunch of nonsense, no? That's the point. I then get rid of any repeating numbers, so my numerical combination looks like this:

**465731298**

From there, I draw a circle, a lot like a clock face, except instead of numbers 1–12, I use number 1–9. Your circle doesn't have to be perfect, just coherent. From there, I draw lines between the numbers in the order I received, creating a pattern or shape within the circle. For example, I would draw a line from four to six, then six to five, then five to seven, and so on and so forth. I like my sigils to look different depending on their use. For banishing sigils or sigils to do harm, I like making the lines straight, with little points on the ends and lots of overlap. For protection sigils, I like more circular, soft shapes, so I may curve a line between numbers, add circles or half-circles to the edges of lines, or otherwise make the sigil look "friendlier" to me. From there, I draw the sigil into my book of shadows and write the general meaning (never the specific, to assist me in forgetting it).

The last three letters of Hine's acronym concern the ways of pushing the sigil out into the universe:

### Intense gnosis/Indifferent vacuity

Either an act of gnosis, or magickal ritual. The other example is through indifferent vacuity, or a "non-bothered" state, like drawing sigils in a workbook at school, or incorporating them into other artistic endeavors.

### Fire

This is about projecting the sigil outward when it is at its most powerful. Hine gives multiple examples of this, but I actually enjoy using physical fire. I'll charge my sigil whether it be through doodling it, placing it under a crystal, or otherwise having it around, placing fingers on it to give it a little bit of energy, and then burn

it to release it into the universe. You can also, in this way, incorporate sigils into other spells, by creating it, charging it, then releasing it to the universe.

### Forget

After you have let your sigil go out into the universe via your desired method, you forget about it. In a way, it's just allowing the universe (or the void, whichever you prefer) to take control of the spell and carry your intent to fruition.

I like creating sigils for specific purposes, but I've found them to be all the more powerful after they are continuously used for specific spells. I have sigils that I've created for protection, banishing, binding, sleeping, money, and all manner of things—and I always use them. The more I use them, the more power is placed into them, the more they work. I tend to charge my sigil for the first use, and then after the first successful spell, the sigil is given meaning. It is given a purpose, and power, and its continuous use in my spells, in whichever spell it is used for, only continues to feed it that power.

In addition, I tend to use sigils by themselves. I will embroider them into my bandanas to banish negative energy or carry them in my pockets to create luck. I have found sigil magick to be the most reliable form of magick I can find, especially after doing it for several years.

## THE CIRCLE

If you have read any Wiccan books, you will be familiar with the term "calling the quarters," or casting a circle, and, like many tools in this section, you are not required to cast a circle to complete your spell work. The Wiccan "calling the quarters" originates from the neo-Enochian Golden Dawn system, specifically pulling influences from certain ceremonial rites such as the Greater Ritual of the Hexagram. The traditional Wiccan circle casting of Gerald Gardner, which can be found in *The Gardnerian Book of Shadows*, will look slightly different to more eclectic Wiccan renditions of the rite. There are many different renditions and ways to call a circle. A similar type of ritual to prep for spell work is discussed in Gemma Gary's *Traditional Witchcraft* with a different purpose. Circle casting is also found in several ceremonial magicks and is used to keep energies in rather than keep energies out within different traditions. For example, in Solomic magick the circle is used to protect the caster, and the concept of "circles" primarily comes from the idea of evocation that was then expanded upon and evolved into the approach that is used widely within Western magickal practice. The method you use to cast a circle may vary from the one your other friends of the Craft employ. In Wicca, the circle is cast before every ceremony, calling in the various elements from their due direction to assist in protection during the ritual (Cunningham, 2009). In traditional Cornish folk craft, rather than having a circle, there is a space known as the Witches' Compass that is a place to invoke powers and spirits of the different directions. Instead of four directions, there are seven recognized: north, south, east, west, above, below, and the seventh, a mystery—the center where all is one. It is also known as the Round of the Wise, Compass Round, created by acts of walking the round, mill dances, and mill chants (Gary, 2008).

If you choose to cast a circle as part of your craft, the method you use to do so is very much up to you, as is the purpose of casting the circle. For my larger spells, I do often choose to cast a circle. I have used the same method of calling in the quarters for assistance in spell work for around seven years, which I have outlined on the following pages. If I feel that calling in the quarters is not as necessary, I will use my wand to draw protective sigils in the air around me, or place items I consider sacred, like crystals and deer antler sheds, in a protective manner around the spell-casting space. In a classic quarter calling, there is often a physical representation of each element in some form.

## CALLING THE QUARTERS/CASTING A CIRCLE

Calling the quarters is the act of calling in the four elements to assist in spell work. The quarters can be called with a finger, wand, or scissors/athame to create the energetic field in the order listed below. The finger and scissors to create a field are not found in classic circle casting but are an accessible option for those without tools from the traditional method. These tools can also be used to actually draw a physical circle by tracing a circle in the air or drawing one in the dirt on the ground to create the shape, thus creating a legitimate area in which you can complete your spell work. Some traditions, such as Alexandrian Wicca, have more specifications than I have listed here. These can include various names of deities written on the circle, a specification in the size of circle, or a difference in objects and their placements to represent the elements.

I often create a circle with crystals or bones, so that when I call the quarters I have a legitimate circle functioning to keep energies in, or to keep energies out during spell work as well. In order to tell which way is which between the four "quarters" and their directions, I will often use a compass on my phone. A note that my directions, instead of pulling from the traditional ceremonial rites, place fire in the east, where the sun rises each morning, thus air in the south. This comes from the influence of my Italian teacher of witchcraft and folk magick and I have implemented it into my practice accordingly.

The six directions and their corresponding elements/forces:

+ **EAST OR FIRE**, signifying action and transformation, anger, creation, and passion. Represented by flame, heated objects. Rules over the tool of the wand and knife.

+ **SOUTH OR AIR**, signifying the mental realm, creativity, invention, inspiration. Represented by feathers, incense, flowers.

+ **WEST OR WATER**, signifying flow, emotions, meditation, introspection, dreams. Represented by shells and cups or bowls of water. Rules over the tool of the cup or chalice.

+ **NORTH OR EARTH**, signifying foundation, grounding, wisdom, prosperity. Represented by salt, soil, oil, and rocks. Rules over the tool of the pentacle.

+ **ABOVE**, the celestial.

+ **BELOW**, the mundane.

Now cast your circle:

1. Start in the east, work clockwise in this order to open the circle: east —> south —> west —> north. Use the tool (finger, scissors, wand, athame) to point in the direction of the east, say the specific elemental incantation for that corner, then move slowly to the south, where you repeat this same rite.

2. Collect an item to represent each element. In this case, it's helpful to use a wand, athame, or a finger to draw the energetic

field you will be working within. If you are invoking (a method of calling on for assistance) gods or spirits, use an invocation familiar to them, a prayer, and/or light a candle in their name after creating the circle.

3. Place the item representing the element in its ruled direction. For example, a feather, representing air, would be placed in the direction of the south. For the above and below, I like to keep bones in my circle, either in the center or on the edges. To me, bones represent something alive that has passed, something that once was within our mundane realm but is now passed over into the celestial. I prefer to use bones of animals that are connected to the specific deities or spirits I am working with, like stag antlers, rabbit heels, or fox teeth.

4. Begin your invocation to the elements. While reciting this invocation, make sure your hand or wand is hovering over or touching the item that corresponds to the element that rules over it—as you invoke and call that quarter.

*All Hail the Watchtower of the (east/south/west/north).*
*The element of (fire/air/water/earth).*
*I do summon and call you forth to guard and protect*
*this circle.*
*Be here, now.*

5. After invoking all of the elements, I use either a deer thigh bone or my wand to hold directly above my head, reciting "as above," then bring the wand or bone directly to the ground in between my feet, reciting "so below." I then begin my spell work.

6. After the spell, I complete the same gesture with the same incantation.

7. To close the circle, work in the reverse order. Instead of circling around from east to north, circle from north to east.

8. To banish the elements, recite this chant:

   *Element of (fire/air/water/earth),*
   *Thank you for your protection.*
   *Return now to the realm from where you came, harming*
   *none along the way, be it men nor beast.*
   *May there be peace between me and thee forever.*
   *Hail and Farewell!*

# MEDITATION

**B**efore spell work takes place, understanding how to cast a spell and especially refining your focus and knowing some of the many methods of transmitting your intent to the universe is essential. The Basis of Spellcraft (see page 17) discusses the idea and use of energy, and how to start getting in touch with it—from there, we open the doors to meditation, grounding, and manipulating energy. Among the most integral parts of witchcraft, these three skills lay the foundation for any and all spell work you will do. Meditation not only helps us get more comfortable sitting with ourselves but also allows us to connect to the universe on a higher level.

Meditating has become, for the most part, one of the key aspects of Western witchcraft. I have not met a witch who does not discuss meditation as something they do frequently—whether they are good or bad at it. For all its uses within witchcraft, I feel there is little to no valuable information on it in modern-day witchcraft books. Before explaining a bit about what meditation is to me, it must be noted that this practice was first recorded in the Vedas scriptures in around 1500 BCE, and is an integral part of many religions, such as Hinduism, Buddhism, Judaism, and Sikhism, serving various purposes. To truly understand meditation, it's best to learn from the masters themselves and really look into its importance and uses in Hinduism, Buddhism, and other Eastern-based religions.

Meditation, in basic terms, is a way of focusing energy and bringing awareness to your energy and self until a clear, stable mindset is met. In the Vedas, meditation is referred to as *dhyāna*, used in yoga exercises and as a way to self-knowledge. Within Western and modern-day witchcraft, and within my practice, meditation is used to help bring focus and awareness to my emotions, whether they be good or bad. It's an essential step before spell work, helping to balance your energy and harness it before casting. Meditating is a way to allow the practitioner to get more in touch with the self and the energy of the self, opening a gateway into more advanced practices like astral projection, trance work, and shadow work. The Basis of Spellcraft illustrates a meditation technique using breath to understand energy, but, as many practitioners have difficulty sitting still, this section will discuss active meditation to portray the different ways that a practitioner can get in touch with their energy.

For active meditation, it's important to do something that allows you to "check out"—I do not recommend doing active meditation when your awareness needs to be present on your task, so please do not try this while driving or tackling something that could injure you if done incorrectly. Although a lot of people see meditation as just "zoning out," or clearing your mind, it is more about awareness and reining in focus. I like doing my active meditation during physical activities, like yoga or a hike, or when doing something creative, like painting or drawing. Active meditation can also be done in the bath or shower, or with practically anything that allows you to intuitively or creatively connect with your energy. If you have no experience whatsoever in active meditation, I urge you to try the exercise on the following page.

As you continue working and doing meditation, whether it is active or not, you will be able to slip into a meditative state more easily, which allows room for those more advanced practices mentioned above. This, like the breathing exercise, brings an essence of mindfulness to your energy—how it interacts within your body and with other objects and how it feels. For me, an empath, this is my energy signature. After practicing meditation for years, it becomes much easier for me to tune in to the energies of other entities and people. I can easily sort through my emotions versus their emotions and understand when I am picking up on the feelings and moods of others and mirroring them. It allows me to feel more keenly when a spirit, deity, or other entity is present in my space, and from there my practice has become more advanced.

As a building block, meditation is imperative to all aspects of the Craft, whether you are just starting out or working toward more advanced practices. Even if you feel like you aren't ready to explore witchcraft quite yet, meditation is a great way to become more self-aware and get in touch with your body and mind.

# Meditation exercise

*Put on some comfy clothes if you have them, but leave your feet bare. This exercise can be done inside or outside, although I prefer to do it outside. It's best done in a more open space, or a space you are familiar with to avoid running into things.*

*Spend some time walking around your space—is it big or small? Is it cramped or spacious? Is it open to daylight, or closed off and slightly darker?*

*Allow yourself to touch the items and things within the space that you feel drawn to. This can be a plant, an old checkerboard, a vase, a fridge or bed, anything in your area. If you're outside, touch the trees, the plants in the yard, and any pets that may be outside with you.*

*As you begin to get more settled in your space, understanding how it feels and what it looks like, allow yourself to zone out while you walk. Let your body continue moving in the space, but allow your mind to drift off. Think about the motions of your muscles and joints and how they're assisting you. Think about the beating of your heart, the heavy inhale and exhale of your lungs, and where your mind wanders.*

*Draw your attention from the objects and your external world to the internal—what is stressing you out today? What are you happy about? What has been on your mind?*

As these thoughts come to you, allow them to linger, then actively let them go.

Bring your attention more to the way you conduct yourself in the space, the way you breathe, and the way your body holds itself. Where do you feel tension? Where do you feel an abundance of energy?

If you feel tired of walking, you can stretch instead, still bringing awareness to your body and energy, and nurturing the areas that feel like they have been ignored. For me, this is often my lower back, feet, and stomach, so I will take time stretching them out and massaging them during this exercise.

If you feel comfortable while stretching, you can close your eyes. Your awareness should remain, if not completely then mostly, on your body and mind.

# GROUNDING

From meditation, we move into what practitioners of the Craft call grounding. This is the act of bringing down your energy, before and after spell casting, to balance yourself and reconnect to the material realm. Grounding is an important sub-aspect of meditation, serving to help focus our energy and keep connected to our plane of existence. Without grounding, we can get lost in spirituality or spell work, and lose an understanding of what is real and not real. Grounding is also an important facet of psychology, helping someone reorient and stay in the present when feeling overwhelmed or dissociated, and keeping someone from an intense emotional state.

Like meditation, grounding can be done in a variety of ways. At the end of this section, there is a particular grounding exercise that I enjoy. In essence, grounding is about connecting or reconnecting with the earthly plane. Like the rest of witchcraft, the way that a practitioner chooses to ground is entirely personal to them. Some will choose to eat or drink before and after rituals to bring themselves back down to the material world, or to walk barefoot to feel the earth beneath their feet. Some practitioners may touch plants or animals to ground.

Grounding is not just a magickal practice but a mundane one. It's a reminder to consistently humble ourselves in the Craft, to stay close to the edge of the material realm, science, and logic. Within magick, there are laws. Although your practice is personal and the magick and methods you use are up to you, the rules of the earth, physics, and science still apply to the Craft. For example, witches in movies and TV shows blithely demonstrate levitation as one of the easiest spells. With a quick swish and flick, something is lifted into midair. Real witchcraft abides by gravity—if you are levitating something, it is because you are throwing it up into the air. Although there is some discussion on whether ancient Buddhist monks could levitate items, there has yet to be documentation on levitation in the modern day.

Knowing the limits of your consciousness due to your mortal body is important. The idea that belief is power holds value and helps us in the Craft (if you believe something to be true, it becomes true), but the belief of a single human being versus hundreds of thousands of years of belief (such as belief in the Bible) pales in comparison. Understanding that the power of many versus the power of one, and the power of deities and deity-like entities versus the power of mortals, is imperative to understanding how the Craft can and cannot work. For example, your belief in something may, just like a spell, power a week to a month of change, depending on whether you continue being active in the spell, if your intent is strong, and on the materials you use. Your belief, however, cannot change fundamental laws of the universe or our reality, like the material components of a specific stone. This is without traveling into the realm of quantum physics or theories about telekinesis, psychokinesis, elemental manipulation, etc., but merely the idea that science and magick walk hand in hand. To deny science is to deny magick and, when working within the Craft, understanding your limits as well as the limits of the world around you is incredibly important.

This, in part, is how we ground, and how we can cast spells with more effectiveness. To manipulate energy and get a desired response like we do within the Craft, we have to understand energy completely. This includes the limits of our own energy, as well as the limits of the energy around us.

The exercise opposite is one of my favorites and one that I do relatively frequently if I can. You need no materials, just bare feet and either grass or ground or some solid indoor flooring. This is a physical exercise that I prefer to do standing, but it can also be done sitting or lying down.

This exercise helps me reconnect with the material world, extending my spirit into the physical plane, as well as being a symbolic exercise of "as above, so below" (see page 75).

# Grounding exercise

*To begin, place your feet just over hip-width (the same distance if you are sitting) apart, and press your hands together at your sternum. If you're sitting or lying down, they can be placed beside you, on your stomach, or on your legs. Begin breathing deeply in and out. When you breathe in, feel the swell of your chest and ribs expanding, and when you breathe out, feel the collapse and shrinking of your lungs. When you breathe in, imagine that the air is energy, life-force, green and growing, that gathers in your chest as it settles in your lungs, and when you breathe out, imagine the exhalation pushing the energy out of your feet and fingertips. If you struggle with visualization, continue focusing on your breathing. Feel the weight of your feet as they sink into the floor and the weight of your hands as they lie flat. Feel the way the energy moves within your body—your inhalation bringing energy in, exhalation taking energy out. If you are able to visualize, you can imagine that, as the energy leaves your body, it snakes itself into the ground, becoming roots in the soil. With every breath, the energetic roots from your feet and fingertips push themselves into the ground further. You can also do this exercise with your hands upward, imagining that leaves, twigs, and branches are exiting with each exhale. Steady your core with each cycle of breath, much like a sturdy oak tree, and know your roots and branches cannot be moved.*

# MANIPULATING ENERGY

Throughout the past sections, we've discussed important aspects of understanding witchcraft and spell work. To an extent, these aspects have all been part of manipulating energy, because the Craft is, in essence, just that. Even then, this idea of manipulating energy is more common than most non-practitioners believe. For example, when you know you have a test, you study to get a good grade. You are actively putting work into something in order to influence the outcome. When you know you have a job interview, you prepare a resumé, dress a certain way, and practice questions in order to impress the interviewer, which is also actively putting work into something to influence the outcome. In our everyday lives, there are things that we put energy toward to actively change our paths—we eat so we will not be hungry, we sleep so we will not be tired, manipulating energy in order to create the outcome we desire.

It's the same with spell work and the Craft. We call on our own energy, the energy of the elements, of deities, our ancestors, of forces beyond us, to assist us in bringing forward the outcome we desire. In Christianity, Judaism, Catholicism, and Islam, these ideas still remain—when you wish for assistance, you pray. You attend temple, church, or mosque. You turn to the saints, God, angels, or celestial bodies. You pray the rosary. You anoint with holy water. In witchcraft, this idea is the same, but we call upon our own power. Witches may work with deities, saints, elements, or angels, but those energies are there to provide protection and assistance when necessary. Witchcraft brings control out of divine energies and into your own hands.

This is what brings many people to the Craft. I was brought to it after leaving a relationship where I felt I was devoid of power and control. Yet, I did not truly understand the Craft until years later. What drew me to this path was the idea of controlling things that were not meant to be controlled and I stayed because it helped me bring mindfulness, attention, and awareness to my everyday habits, routines, and thoughts. The true manipulation of energy lies in where you direct it. I structure my days around intent, things that I wish to achieve, and spending time around people I love who treat me the way I deserve. I have worked tirelessly in therapy to learn how to cast out anxious and intrusive thoughts, which I still struggle with and still seek treatment for. I have structured my life around the idea of witchcraft and manipulating energy and the idea that you can think something into existence.

My spells are reserved for when I need an extra push. If I feel like I have done my best, but still want to cover the last base, I will cast. If a friend comes to me seeking justice where the system has failed them, I will cast. If I feel as though my material actions cannot completely satisfy the need of a particular situation, I will cast. Witchcraft is a tool, but it is also a way of life. At the end of the day, whether you put your energy into situations that do not benefit you or the greater good, or make you happy, is your choice, but to be a witch is to choose the path that will assist you and others, even if it's the harder path. It's to become aware of how you structure your time. You don't need a candle or materials to cast certain spells—just an understanding of what you need and how to obtain it. If that requires a votive candle, mugwort, and chili peppers, then that is what it requires. But sometimes, the manipulation of energy is as simple as not answering a text, being aware of your thought processes, and pushing to be your best self.

Manipulating energy is understanding the way you interact with the world, the way the world interacts with you, and how you interact with yourself. Exercises like grounding and meditation assist in this, as does shadow work, but on the opposite page is an energy work exercise that you can do to help you understand energy.

This particular exercise is not created in the hopes of you being "successful" at it but is helping you understand further what helps you, as a practitioner, manipulate and work with the energies around you. Every practitioner casts in different ways. For me, I rely heavily on energy work and visualization, while some work with prayer, and others work with physical movement. It's okay if you don't get it right away, or if you never get it. That only means that this isn't the right exercise for you, and not that you have failed or are a "bad witch." This particular exercise assisted me in understanding the best way for me to work within my spells, and the hope is that it does so for other witches as well.

# Energy work exercise

*Ground yourself. Place your hands out in front of you, almost in a cupped shape. Allow yourself to breathe in and out, and feel with every exhalation that the energy from your breath is gathered into your hands. If you can visualize, imagine a small ball of light forming in between your palms.*

*If you have aphantasia, or trouble visualizing, allow yourself to move your hands in whichever which way you like, and feel the energy gather from your movement and breathing.*

*When you feel as though your energy has collected to the greatest of its ability, you can either let it disperse, or use this collected energy to charge something. If you choose to charge something, feel free to touch your hand to an object and state what the energy may be used for.*

When you feel ready to attempt your first spell, which can be any time from within your first few months to the first year, I recommend choosing and creating something simple. Choose something that resonates with you, and explore all the different methods for casting—candles, satchels, jars—to find what best fits the intent. I recommend writing down the spell beforehand so you don't forget it, and if you want you can plan it according to the lunar phases or days of the week.

Below is a quick synopsis of how the moon cycles and the days of the week assist us in our casting.

## THE DAYS OF THE WEEK

### Sunday

Ruled by the sun and divine outer world/active energy. Sunday is a great day to cast spells related to your career, success, personal goals, growth, and healing.

**EXAMPLE SPELL:** Success spells, manifesting goals, healing spells, writing down and beginning manifestations toward goals.

### Monday

Ruled by the moon. Monday is a great day to cast spells for family matters, psychic powers, emotions, or intuitive work.

**EXAMPLE SPELL:** Working on psychic powers, manifestation in the emotional realm, spells to assist in intuition.

## Tuesday

Ruled by Mars, the notorious Roman god of war, this is a great day to cast spells for courage, men, sex, banishing/binding, curses, and hex breaking.

**EXAMPLE SPELL:** Courage, an unbinding, uncrossing bath.

## Wednesday

Ruled by Mercury. Wednesday is a great day to cast spells for communication, education, travel, and creativity.

**EXAMPLE SPELL:** Focus, doing well on a specific test, opening communication with someone.

## Thursday

Ruled by Jupiter. Thursday is a great day to cast spells for wealth, abundance, legal affairs, and business, as well as political power.

**EXAMPLE SPELL:** Justice, money, winning a court case.

## Friday

Ruled by Venus. Friday is a great day to cast spells for beauty, love, fertility, and anything pertaining to nature.

**EXAMPLE SPELL:** Self-love, glamour.

## Saturday

Ruled by Saturn. Saturday is a great day to cast spells for protection, obstacles, removing road blocks, cleansing, or endings.

**EXAMPLE SPELL:** Unbinding, uncrossing, protection.

## THE LUNAR CYCLES

*There are thirteen full moons every year that assist with different things. Here I will be covering the actual cycles of the moon, not the full moons themselves.*

**FULL MOON:** For all-purpose magick, love, charging, healing, cleansing, clarity.

### Phases to repel

**WANING CRESCENT:** For clearing your life of negativity, banishments, balance, ending, and atonement.

**WANING HALF-MOON:** For obstacles, temptations, transitions, breaking bad habits, and banishing.

**WANING GIBBOUS:** For introspection, banishing, cleansing of objects, undoing bindings, cursing.

**NEW MOON:** For destructive magick, banishment, divination, cleansing, and fertility.

### Phases to attract

**WAXING GIBBOUS:** For success, good health, renewal, power boost, constructive magick.

**WAXING HALF-MOON:** For strength, motivation, divination, creativity, attraction, bonding.

**WAXING CRESCENT:** For luck, magick for yourself, positivity, conjuring, passion, and wealth.

Whether you decide to use the lunar cycles and the days of the week to assist you or not is your choice as a practitioner, but if you're looking for that extra boost on a binding or a little bit more energy behind a wealth spell, timing it to the appropriate day of the week or to a corresponding lunar cycle is extremely helpful.

Understand that this is your first spell, and it may not go as planned or may not work. If it does, note what you can improve on—did it manifest in strange ways? Did it play out the way you wished? If it doesn't, look over your spell—where do you feel you went wrong? Do you feel like this method wasn't right for you? Part of being a modern witch is understanding that we are always learning, growing, and changing, like the seasons and the moon. There is no stagnancy in witchcraft, and mistakes are bound to happen. Oftentimes, the mistakes are what help us learn. They give us experience in how we went wrong, so we know then what does not work for us. Understanding our flaws and taking criticism is another important aspect of witchcraft—one that we continue to do throughout our whole lives and practices, usually through the method of shadow work.

# SHADOW WORK

S hadow work, which is considered a relatively large part of witchcraft at any stage, is actually a psychological concept by Carl Jung. The idea is based around the shadow self, or the self that we repress, hate, and reject, all the flaws and emotions we consider "negative," like anger, sadness, fear, jealousy. When we ignore and push down these aspects, they become part of the shadow self. They are disowned and unexamined, and tend to become bigger when we avoid them.

Notions of "good" and "bad" are undoubtedly human, but, of these polarities, we often ignore and subdue the emotions we consider "bad." These can be fear, anger, envy, hate, or what many psychologists, including Carl Jung, consider "primitive" human emotions. An abundance of certain shadow aspects creates an imbalance, where witchcraft strives to attain balance. We have labeled certain traits and characteristics as "good" because they fit into our ego—another thing the Jungian psychology addresses—when they may be sourced from trauma, or cause us to lash out in ways that we feel really aren't like us. Among the things that often emerge when we repress our shadow selves are judgment of ourselves and others, blame, anger, and projection. Carl Jung writes in *Psychology and Religion* (1938), "But if it is repressed and isolated from consciousness, it never gets corrected." Our self-doubt about whether or not we are a "bad" person surfaces when we hurt ourselves, hurt others, or do something that feels so incredibly unlike us. For more on shadow work, see page 152.

# PART 3

# MANIFESTING CHANGE THROUGH WITCHCRAFT

# CLEANSING AND PROTECTING SPACES

## CLEANSING

When you hear a witch say something along the lines of, "You need to cleanse" or "Have you cleansed yourself recently?," most of the time this translates to, "Something about your vibe is off." When we discuss negative energies, we are talking about energy that is harmful to the self or the space—for example, parasitic entities, intrusive thoughts, harmful anger (see the shadow work section on pages 98–99, for example). The Craft, ultimately, is about balance between the negative and positive, so when cleansing we try to target the ideas, entities, and energies that are not serving us or are working as an obstacle against us. Not all "negative" energies, like sadness, frustration, anxiety, are necessarily bad if they are coped with in healthy ways, and almost all "negative" energies have a purpose. Those that feed off your pessimism, block your path, or are detrimental to your physical, spiritual, and mental health are the ones that we opt to remove.

Cleansing and understanding cleansing is one of the baseline rituals a practitioner can and should form before learning to cast spells. In the Craft, cleansing is seen as cleaning. It is spiritual and energetic upkeep, and an essential part of making sure your space and your energy stay where you want them to be. Just as a house that hasn't been vacuumed, dusted, or swept begins to gather dirt and grime, an uncleansed home is prone to collecting energy in the same way and cleansing keeps your space in top shape. Areas that are frequently used by members of the household are the most energetically active, just like areas that are never touched will be stagnant. Sometimes this energy that has collected can be negative or malicious, or sometimes it can just be neutral. I usually refer to neutral energy as "energetic clutter." Either way, there are many different methods of cleansing, as well as different times to cleanse.

To those unfamiliar with the Craft, I often use this metaphor to describe the importance of cleansing and cleansing regularly. Let's say you go to the park. You fall, or someone pushes you over. When this happens, you get dirt on both your hands and your clothes. When you go home, do you wash it off? Or do you leave the dirt for days, even weeks, on your jeans and hands? When we come into contact with something negative, whether that be a person, energy, or entity, we need to cleanse ourselves. This "dirty energy" can be placed on you, in situations where someone is thinking ill of you, which is sometimes referred to as the "evil eye." It can also linger in spaces, for example when someone in your household gets angry, or someone disrespectful comes over. The energy can even be transferred to you when you go out somewhere, if the place in question has lingering energy. All of the places you have been to or inhabit, as well as all of the people you meet, have the possibility of transferring "dirty energy" on to you. Most of the time, it's not even a conscious choice, which is why many practitioners cleanse. As your intuition gets stronger, you'll notice which people give off certain energies, or "vibes," and what areas of the home seem most prone to collecting stagnant energy.

Personally, I like to cleanse every week or so. I consider this a baseline cleansing, to keep unwanted energies out of my personal space. I prefer to smoke-cleanse with sandalwood, rosemary, or frankincense, and carry the incense stick, wood, or herb bundle around my home to rid it of unnecessary energetic clutter. Once a month, I'll deep-cleanse my windowsills, altar spaces, bedsheets, and desktop. These are the areas where I am the most spiritually or physically active, like sleeping, working, or doing spell work. I find that energetic clutter in these spaces affects me the most, making me run-down, prone to headaches, and laziness. I like to cleanse myself weekly, but I do take cleansing/uncrossing baths on those deep-cleansing days. If I find that a negative entity is present, either by feeling a change in the energy of the house or by noticing some of my protections are acting strangely, I'll use sleigh bells to clear out the space. Before any spell work, I cleanse at least my hands in case there is something lingering on them.

Every witch is different regarding how often and how they cleanse. I know witches who will cleanse before a spell, who will cleanse in a smaller way every day, and who will cleanse every other week. How you cleanse and when you cleanse is completely up to the practitioner.

Something to consider when cleansing is the debate concerning white sage. White sage, or *Salvia apiana,* is a North American herb that is sacred to indigenous peoples and tribes. The sacred plant, which First Nations have been using for generations, is now almost completely out of reach because of its overuse by non-indigenous occult practitioners. In the same vein, "smudging," which is a specific ritual that you have to learn in indigenous culture, is now synonymous with "smoke cleansing," which is a falsehood that many practitioners have been working to eradicate within the occult community.

This is not to say that smoke cleansing is off limits—only the use of white sage and calling your smoke cleansing "smudging." In the same way, *palo santo*, another herb used by the indigenous people of South America, has been colonized and appropriated, far removed from the original rituals and spiritual traditions. You might be thinking, "Who cares! It grows from the earth." In the words of my indigenous friend, Owen, the problem with cultural appropriation is as follows: "Treating the culture as a costume or picking it apart for selfish gains not only insults but erases the culture as a whole, possibly doing unfixable damage and changing cultural narratives." For more on why I encourage you to conduct further research into the use of white sage and *palo santo*, see page 172.

In most cases, white sage isn't what you would want to use to cleanse. It acts as a bleach, erasing *all* energies from the area, positive and negative. When creating a place of power, like an altar or desk, where spell work or other work is routinely done, erasing all energies and reminders of energies isn't necessarily what you want. When smoke cleansing to remove all negative energies and entities, I often use rosemary, mugwort, cedar, or frankincense—all of which have protective and purifying properties.

In the same way that we cleanse with smoke, fire, water, we also need to cleanse our lives. When feeling stuck or stagnant, take some time to reflect on your energy and the energy around you. Are there people in your life who don't treat you the way you deserve? Are there physical items stacked in the corners of your space that hold weight? What are you holding on to, physically or emotionally, that is dragging you down and working as deadweight? Are you ignoring and rejecting emotions, pushing them down and compartmentalizing, refusing to acknowledge them? In the same way that energy collects, so do our emotions. It's easy for us to slip into comfortable cycles, even if they do not serve us. It's easy for us to project and prod at other people's insecurities, but not our own. When a practitioner cleanses, they cleanse not only their space but their mind and spirit.

# Basic cleansing ritual

*For this ritual, you can use whatever tool for cleansing you like. I recommend bells, pots to bang together, a cedar or rosemary herb bundle, or sandalwood.*

*Begin by either opening your door or windows. Start at the very top of the house, whatever floor that may be, and begin by either lighting your herb bundle or incense, or by beginning to shake your bells. If you live in a one-floor house or apartment, simply start in one area. I like to start at a certain point then move clockwise throughout the house, but you can follow your intuition for this. State your intent, which can be as simple as "I cleanse this space of negativity" or as elaborate as a specific paragraph in multiple languages. Enter the first room on that floor and begin slowly walking around the perimeter of it. You can state your intent over and over, or you can state it only as you enter a new room. Make sure you do this for every room on each floor, moving down slowly and stating the intent every time you need. Make sure you end at the open door, or end your sweep of a room or floor at an open window. If you want, you can thank the energy or spirit for stopping by, and firmly say it may not return again.*

# PROTECTION

In the same vein, protection is imperative as a foundation of witchcraft. When we discuss protection, we do so in extremely broad terms because it is a broad topic. When speaking with clients I tend to marshal the ideas of protection into two categories: Protection of Space (such as warding of hearth) and Protection of Self (protecting energy and spirit). The protection methods I will discuss in this section are methods that anyone and everyone could employ, from wearing protective amulets to warding the home and creating emotional boundaries with the people around you. I keep protection close to cleansing because after we cleanse, we protect—in that order specifically. The idea is to get all the dirty energy out, then keep it from coming back in. There are methods of protection that will be familiar to the non-practitioner and methods of protection that will be familiar to the practitioner, but both should have access to Protection of Space and Protection of Self. For example, a method of protection that the non-practitioner would be familiar with is creating boundaries to protect their energy. A method of protection that the practitioner would be familiar with is a witch bottle, which is a form of warding.

Warding, in itself, is "to ward" something away, whether that be negative energy or a specific type of energy or person. In witchcraft, this can be parasitic entities, toxic or abusive people, harmful magick like hexes, jinxes, curses, or the evil eye. There are a few ways to go about it. We can ward to keep all energy out, which I consider to be indiscriminate warding, or ward to keep only negative energy out, which I consider selective warding. When we indiscriminately ward, it keeps out all energies, including earthbound or passerby spirits, deities, daemons, angels, as well as stereotypically harmful entities. When we selectively ward, it keeps out only entities that are deemed negative or that wish harm upon you or the members of the house. A few examples of warding are:

+ **The witch bottle** (full instructions on how to make this are given on the next page), to serve as a decoy for your energy and being, known to trap spirits and negative entities.

+ **Charm bags and enchanted objects** placed at the doors, which then create a magickal ward at all the entrance points of your home.

+ **Things buried in front yards**, which can often be witch bottles, or other protective methods to keep the harm from ever reaching you and your threshold.

+ **Salt rings for casting circles**, to keep energies in or out while casting spells.

When warding our space, there are different places that need protecting (I encourage you to ward *all* of them), including the full house or living space, your room/personal living space, your altar, and your area where you cast spells. The latter can often be referred to as casting a circle, if you protect during casting, or just regular warding if your casting area is different to your living area. Your altar is typically your place of casting or worship, but not always. Some altars serve only as places of worship, and some are working altars.

Personally, my altar holds my wand, crystals, lighters, tarot cards, and candles for each of my patron deities and saints. I have offerings like bones, insects, crystals, spells all coordinated to each of them, as well as offerings that I frequently switch out, like water, coffee, wine, olive oil, and rum. The protection for my altar comes from a plant, funnily enough, that sits beside my statue of Diana. This particular plant was potted with a charged crystal as well as a symbol/sigil written on a piece of paper that gives the plant a purpose to protect my altar space. Meanwhile, my bed area and room are protected by various charms, including bags, a bundle of echinacea stems tied with cinnamon and a hawk feather, and a protection charm gifted to me by a friend many years ago, hanging over my bedframe. I protect my house in multiple ways. I have a protection candle that, when burned, feeds a ward to my house. I have a ward buried in the four corners of my yard (a sigil on paper, sealed with wax from a candle spell) that catches and reflects any hexes, jinxes, curses, or harmful energy sent my way. I have embroidered cloth bags at each of my house's doors. I have a little jar of war water, known for its temperamental nature, at my front door, made with extreme care and intent to sow discord in the lives of those who might wish to harm me and my family. That's to name just a few, and there are many others that I have placed out of sight, out of mind, in different areas of the yard and house.

There are multiple methods for warding, but the classic and one of my favorites remains the witch bottle. Placed under the bed or buried in the yard, it is a traditional protection method aimed at catching harmful energies and spirits.

# Witch Bottle

*Please note that the traditional version of this bottle uses bodily fluids, such as urine and blood. If you, like me, are squeamish, you can use this slightly altered method. You will need a jar or bottle with a lid.*

## INGREDIENTS:

fingernails and hair

red thread

vinegar

wine

pins or sharp objects (be careful when handling sharp objects, especially needles, pins, or pieces of broken glass)

chili peppers

cloves

thyme

eggshells

sea salt

wormwood

1.  Place all the ingredients in the jar with the intent to protect or capture spirits and energy cast against you.

2.  I don't have a particular chant for this spell, so I encourage you to make your own, or charge each object

with a specific intent. To charge, place the object or ingredient with a sigil and crystal lined up with your intent in a bag (any bag will do, I typically use cloth). Leave for nine days beforehand. I choose nine because it's typically a number of power, but you can also use three, five, seven, or thirteen depending on your beliefs.

3. After placing all the charged ingredients in the jar, close (tightly!) and take a black candle anointed with a protective oil to burn on top. I typically use jars with metal lids to avoid a hole being burned through. If you want, you can put a protective sigil on the candle. I try to use a taper or chime candle. You can also seal the bottle with wax, but depending on the type of jar you're using this could prove difficult. I like to just let my candle burn down.

4. When the candle has finished burning (watch the candle patterns and the way the flame burns for information on how the spell is doing), place the witch bottle in your desired location. For me, that's under my bed. The bottle will need to be replaced when it's "caught" something—the contents may have blackened or darkened, or some kind of mold or fungus will have grown.

Technically, this bottle only protects the person who is a witch, or whose fingernails and hair it contains. For broader protection spells, charm bags or jars placed at doors could be more beneficial for protection of the house. I am a big fan of charm bags, and typically embroider mine with sigils.

An important point to keep in mind is that all protection, especially wards and protective jewelry, has to be recharged unless you tether it to an energy source. I use the term "tethering" loosely, but what it means for the most part is the spell or ward is connected to a specific energy source that continues to charge it without you having to do much. For one of my wards protecting my house, each month I create a candle that, when lit, charges my ward. I do this by writing specific sigils and evocations on the candle itself, and I use the candle every day. However, I know of people who simply perform a small act every day, like touching something or meditating, to recharge their wards. Some people redo their original ritual every month to recharge. Recharging a protective spell has to do with what you are capable of, as a practitioner. As I've advanced in my practice, I've found that simply stating that specific action to recharge one of my wards works wonders, as does giving a little bit of energy to each of my charm bags once a week. Sometimes giving energy looks like a touch or holding it in your hand and sometimes it looks like meditating with the object with the intent of the spell in mind. For one of my wards, I redo my particular spell every month, which involves writing sigils on paper, sealing with wax from a specific spell candle, and burying

in the four corners of my yard. With protective jewelry, I usually clean the charm under water (make sure, if it's crystal jewelry, that it's not water soluble) or place it on salt to cleanse, then restate my intent with a prayer.

Charmed jewelry is one of my favorite methods of protecting the self. My second favorite method is veiling (see pages 131–32), but by far the most attainable method is boundaries. When we talk about boundaries, it is often in loose terms, and if you grew up in America like I did, boundaries aren't always something that people have. If you struggle with boundaries, it's okay! Most people do. Especially with the rise of social media, we often feel as though everyone's lives are ours to consume (think the Kardashians and their fans' investment in their lives). Depending on the type of house you grew up in or the type of relationships you had in your teenage years, you could also struggle with boundaries. Or, simply, you don't like saying no to people. I don't either. When we talk about boundaries in conjunction with magick and the Craft, I often bring up energy. Among the questions I ask my clients are the following:

✛ How's your energy level on a day-to-day basis?

✛ Where do you put your energy?

✛ Do you take time for yourself each day?

✛ Do you maintain relationships with individuals who don't match the energy you put into the relationship?

✛ Do you feel inclined to say yes to people even when you are tired or don't necessarily feel up to helping out or being around them?

These questions center mostly around where you put your energy. Is it being channeled toward people and things that are supporting you, pushing you forward, and benefiting you? Are you putting yourself first? If not, it's time to begin protecting yourself and your energy, prioritizing yourself, and moving forward on the path to self-love.

# THE JOURNEY TO SELF-LOVE AND SELF-PRIORITIZATION

When I talk about self-love and self-prioritization in terms of witchcraft, I don't just mean putting a face mask on or taking a bath and calling it a day. Oftentimes, the self-care we need is not the self-care we want to do, but rather the harder road to follow. When I think about love, I think mostly about the pets my family has. Each animal, whether it's rabbit, cat, or dog, loves very differently from the others. Each one expresses love in their own way. For example, my cat expresses love by sharing space—being in the proximity of someone, whether it's one of the family or another animal, and just being. My dogs express love more outwardly by licking, demanding attention, pawing, or barking. My rabbit expresses love in curiosity—friendly nudges, little paws placed on legs, sniffing feet, hands, and sometimes rubbing her chin on things she has decided are hers. Crucially, each one manages to understand the love of the others. The dogs, even if they can't express the same love, will share space with the cat, or playfully poke at his boundaries, and nudge at the rabbit to show interest. The rabbit will share space with the cat, and the cat will lovingly bat at both. Love and care come to us, naturally, in all sorts of ways—this chapter merely discusses some of them. When exploring how best to take care of yourself or prioritize yourself, know that the way you find self-care and self-prioritization may vary greatly from the way your friend finds them or from the way I find them. Self-love and self-prioritization are, above all, finding out not only what you want in life, from others, and from yourself, but understanding that what you truly need may not always be the same thing.

In the section on protection, I briefly touched on boundaries. When we discuss self-love and self-prioritization, the idea of boundaries comes further into focus.

Personally, I struggled with boundaries and self-esteem issues consistently through my high school and college years because of different forms of mental illness and trauma. Despite growing up in a healthy household that encouraged respecting space and critical thinking, I still internalized the idea that giving my all to something, whether that be a project or a person, would result in positivity. I would throw myself into things and create attachments to people or projects, subconsciously putting my value of self into the validation I received from that, whether it was affection or a good grade.

As I delved further into my craft, the way that I received validation and how much of my self-esteem banked on other people's opinions of me were brought to the forefront. I started noticing how much I cared when someone thought ill of me. I started noticing how I sought out relationships because I felt discomfort with being alone. I was hyper-aware of where I placed my energy on a daily basis, especially since I had a habit of being a people-pleaser and giving kindness and care to those who didn't deserve it. If I am to be completely honest, this is still something I struggle with, a whole seven years into my craft. I still have to be mindful of where I place my energy, and of whether my prioritization of self is where it needs to be.

Witchcraft, as much as it is a form of balance and activism, is a form of empowerment. It brings aspects of both control and mindfulness into your daily life, and helps you create the life you truly desire. In some ways, witchcraft also allows us to understand the things we cannot control. We can't control what other people do or how they treat us, only how we react to it. We cannot control what people say about us, only what we say about them. The Craft brings into focus the things that you may have been ignoring, instead choosing to concentrate on the unavoidable or the unchangeable. When we learn about our energy through meditation and grounding, we can see where it is being channeled and not reciprocated. Witches' energy is precious and helps us cast our spells and succeed, so when it's being taken advantage of, there's a need to set a boundary. In the same way, spirituality has always been used as a means to move toward your higher self, or achieve enlightenment. Although not everyone may be able to devote their entire lives to spirituality, witchcraft helps us look and see where we can give more to ourselves, and in turn, more to others.

A friend of mine often tells me that you cannot heal the world or others without first healing yourself. When you're struggling, or burned out, or overwhelmed, you cannot continue to attempt to help people without first helping yourself. The question becomes this: in a capitalist society where self-care is a luxury, how do we prioritize our needs that go beyond the bare minimum? Society conditions women, those who present as women, and minorities to be accommodating, to please the people around us, and many of my clients often put themselves into a caretaker role. How can we complete self-love and self-prioritization in a way that is accessible to minimum-wage workers, stay-at-home mothers with multiple kids, and those who are focused on making enough money to put food on the table? This is less of a question I can answer, and more of a question I pose to the reader.

Unlike what social media tells you, you don't need materials to self-prioritize. Self-prioritization can be as simple as saying no to doing something unnecessary when you are low on energy. It can also be saying yes to doing something necessary for your mental health when you are low on energy. It can be making sure you and everyone in your household is fed for the day, or getting a good night's sleep. It can be stirring your coffee clockwise to bring in positivity, or counterclockwise to banish negativity.

When encouraging people to put themselves first, I often give them a checklist of things to ask themselves.

✛ What is something you enjoy doing for yourself? (There is no wrong answer to this, it truly can be anything.)

✛ Have you done something that you enjoy doing lately?

✛ Is it possible for you to do something for yourself every day, no matter how small?

✛ How do you talk to yourself? If you talked the way you talk to yourself to a friend, or a friend talked to you the way you talk to yourself, would you be friends with them?

✛ How does your energy interact with others? Do you often find yourself giving more than receiving, starting conversations, or going out of the way to assist and accommodate others when they may not do the same for you?

✛ What boundaries do you have in place to ensure your emotional, mental, and physical health stay the best they can be?

These six questions, which I also ask myself often, bring conscious awareness to how you are interacting with the world around you, and with yourself. I haven't met a single person, client or friend, who hasn't struggled to believe that they deserve the best and who doesn't struggle with self-criticism or self-doubt. That's what society has taught us—to be accommodating, kind above all, and accessible to the people around us. If you're like me and have a tendency to be a healer, you'll find that it's harder to set boundaries with people you want to help.

There is strength in being kind and using the Craft to help others, but, in the same vein, you can be kind while standing up for yourself and reinforcing boundaries. Boundaries protect you and your energy, whether it be with family, in love, or in friendships. To understand your own boundaries, use the following exercise:

# Boundaries exercise

1. *Make a list with three sections: green, yellow, and red.*

2. *Under the green section, write things you are okay with someone doing in a relationship, friendship, or family situation.*

   *For example, my green area includes spotty texting, someone canceling a date, or difficulties communicating. These are things that some may not be okay with, but I personally have no problem within my friendships, relationships, and family situation.*

3. *Under the yellow section, write things you are less okay with someone doing in a relationship, friendship, or family situation.*

   *For example, my yellow area includes someone getting angry at me for no reason. When this happens, it's not necessarily a deal-breaker, but it is something I don't tolerate and will communicate to them that I don't like it. If they do it more than once, or it becomes a pattern, then it becomes a problem and I either re-establish the boundary or try to remove myself from the situation.*

4.   *Under the red section, write things you are* absolutely not okay *with someone doing in a relationship, friendship, or family situation.*

*For example, my red area includes lying. If someone lies to me, I don't typically continue the relationship or friendship. If it's a family member, I remove myself from the situation or lessen contact with them.*

*This exercise is fluid. Your list will change as you become more confident in yourself and begin to tolerate fewer harmful behaviors from people. Mine has changed a great deal since I originally started the exercise, and I'm still working on my boundaries and my relationships with the people around me.*

Journeying to self-love and self-prioritization isn't something that will happen overnight. I'm convinced that it will take years, if not my whole life, to learn how to completely prioritize myself. As new responsibilities emerge, new friendships and relationships, you start over again with setting boundaries and demanding respect. As in witchcraft, there are continuous changes and balance must be upheld. Whether that balance is between time to yourself and time with others, work and your normal life, or family time and alone time, making sure you are at the center of the conversation is imperative. Prioritizing yourself not only assists you in bringing in better things for the universe, but this internal work around your thoughts, doubts, and criticisms of yourself is heavily ingrained in shadow work. In order to become our best selves, there's a level of self-acceptance and inner work we need to do.

Prioritizing yourself, your time, and your energy allows you more room to look into what witchcraft means to you, as well as exploring your comfort zone and beliefs when it comes to the Craft. Your self-love translates into belief and confidence, which in turn bolsters your craft and the power of your spells. When clients come to me wondering why spells aren't working, I often ask them if they *believe* they will work. Doubts about your self and your practice can sometimes, not always, translate into difficulties with spells taking hold. Witchcraft is at its most potent when the caster not only casts effectively but takes action and puts continuous energy and belief behind the spell. Self-love and self-prioritization also allow practitioners to be able to focus more on their craft and spiritual growth.

Witchcraft often asks us not only to see things from an intuitive perspective but to see things from an objective perspective. When I talk about this, I mean that sometimes the thing that you want is not always the thing that you need, and the Craft forces us, before each spell, to analyze whether what we seek is truly something we need and something that will better either ourselves or the community around us. Historically, witches were healers or community leaders who people consulted to receive blessings, help with love or money, and curse removals. They provided protection and divination to help people understand a situation. In Cornwall, these individuals were known as *pellars*, as Gemma Gary explores in her book *Traditional Witchcraft*. In Calabria, Italian folk healers were known as *maghi* or *maghe*, armed with an extensive knowledge of herbs, the ability to treat minor illnesses, and popular magick, as well as Roman Catholicism. Sometimes, they are referred to as *fattucchiere*, or fixers (Kippner and Bova, 2011).

Whether you decide to follow the path of a healer or folk witch is your choice. Even without taking the path of one who helps others, the self remains an imperative part of our craft—it is the most important tool, the source of your energy and power that fuels your spells, and, most of all, it's you. You are important. Self-love and self-prioritization remain an integral part of the Craft, not only to move blockages around your self-doubt and your craft but to be able to differentiate between your desires fueling your shadow self and your needs fueling your higher self.

# Self-love + Healing Satchel

*This spell is used to assist in bringing in more love and passion into your life, to heighten your confidence, and help you heal from any recent hurt that has been brought against you. Be wary that a self-love spell may not always manifest the way you want, and in order to truly manifest self-love there's a need for active work in that area.*

## MATERIALS:

rose quartz chips or stone

cinnamon (sticks are preferable)

rose petals

juniper

blue or pink candle

hibiscus

mugwort

velvet or fabric satchel in the color of your choice

1.  Inscribe the candle with your intent—whether that is healing or self-love, or both. If you want, you can create a specific sigil using the method given in the materials section.

2.  Take the satchel and consecrate it by blessing it or cleansing it with smoke or water.

3. Place each item into the bag, and, as you do so, recite the following chant:

   *With each herb and crystal I place unto thee,*
   *I ask of you to bring me these things three.*
   *When I hold you in my hand,*
   *or place you on my nightstand—*
   *I love myself like the depths of the sea,*
   *I heal from all harm done to me.*
   *When I hold you near,*
   *Be a constant reminder that I am here,*
   *I am confident and I am proud,*
   *Unapologetically loved by myself despite my doubt.*
   (This chant was written at the ripe age of sixteen. If you find it too cheesy, feel free to make your own.)

4. Light the candle with a similar intent, and seal the bag with the wax from the candle, or simply drip some of the wax into the satchel. Let the candle burn down in a safe place.

5. Carry the satchel with you when you need a boost of confidence, or keep it in your personal area for assistance through shadow work and self-love. Personally, I like to carry my self-love satchel with me to therapy appointments or hold it in my hand while I do affirmations for myself.

# Self-Love Mirror Spell

*This ritual can be performed while doing your makeup, stating positive affirmations, or even just washing your face and getting ready for the day.*

## MATERIALS:

an expo marker or another item to draw on a mirror with
   (e.g., lipstick)
mirror

1.   Bless your mirror or consecrate it by drawing a protective sigil with moon water or olive oil on the back.

2.   In the formation of a circle, write compliments to yourself around where your face is. These can be positive affirmations like "I am strong" or "I am beautiful." Write these with the intention of boosting your confidence.

3.   Use the circle of compliments while doing your makeup, stating positive affirmations, or just washing your face and getting ready for the day.

4.   You can leave the circle of compliments up as a helpful spell for every time you use the mirror, or update them every time you want to redo the spell.

# BANISHING
# UNWANTED ENERGY

The one piece of advice that I give to both my mentees and my clients is this: "Never cast a spell you don't know how to undo." I consider banishing an offensive magick and the first step in learning how to undo mistakes. When we are actively practicing witchcraft, banishing is another crucial aspect. Banishing, similar to cleansing, is what we do when things have gone wrong. By that I mean, when your cleansing fails, or your protection wasn't as strong as you thought, how do you more fully get rid of parasitic or negative entities in your space? Banishing as a part of the Craft and also a part of our daily life is important to properly understand. While cleansing is much like cleaning a space, or a spiritual sweep, banishing is like targeting a specific, stubborn stain that refuses to be removed.

The first way to learn about banishing rituals is by looking into the LBRP (Lesser Banishing Ritual of the Pentagram) in the Hermetic Order of the Golden Dawn—by far the most well-known ritual for banishing. The goal of the ritual, like most banishing rituals, is to

clear you and your space of negative energy. The LBRP is done at least once a day by some ceremonialists for a whole year (Miller, 2006) and has been adapted by many other ceremonial and Western mystic groups as it grew in popularity.

Banishing is a method we use when we want to be more thoroughly rid of something that has been plaguing us, whether that's a toxic friend, an entity attached to us, or a negative energy. I typically use banishing in conjunction with binding and/or protection, and there are many different ways to complete a successful banishing spell. Some practitioners like to do a banishing bath, some prefer candle spells, and some even go as far as targeting the specific entity or energy by name to remove them from their lives. While cleansing helps us with spiritual upkeep and tidiness, banishing allows us to more fully protect ourselves, sever ties, and remove road blocks in our paths.

Although banishing is similar to both protective and cleansing spells, the intent changes slightly. Protection spells are used to keep negative energies and entities out, while banishing is more focused on removing something that is already within the space. You may even notice that as your protective methods become more advanced, you have to banish less and less. I tend to do a specific banishing ritual every month, or every couple of weeks, to ensure that my sacred spaces and home stay protected and safe from any possible parasitic entities and negative energy.

I've known certain practitioners to target their banishing spells at specific friends or people they wish to disconnect from, and other practitioners to target their banishing spells at a more general negative entity. Like other spells, it's imperative to be specific in your intent. The particular banishing spell I use is called a "return to sender," aimed at targeting and returning any baneful magick, or harmful magick like hexes, curses, and jinxes, that could be sent toward me or my household. Over time, this ritual became commonplace for me to do every full moon and I even integrated it into my wards to keep away harmful energy. Any energy that is unwanted in your space can be banished. When it comes to banishing, I once again put emphasis on boundaries. I like to ask myself and my clients the following questions:

+ Has someone upset you one too many times?

+ Has an entity made themselves too comfortable in your space?

+ Do you feel like you're being dragged down by other people's emotions?

+ Are the rules you set being disregarded by a spiritual or physical presence?

+ Do you feel there is a negativity in your space that doesn't seem to dissipate even after you cleanse?

When these questions come up in a reading or a mentoring session and are answered yes, I usually recommend a banishing. A consistent method of both banishing and protection that I use is referred to as veiling. This is used for multiple reasons, including religious reasons or protective reasons. When you veil, you place something over the top of your head to shield your energy from other people's energy.

I typically use bandanas, but hats or other garments intended for veiling can be used. I've known some empaths who use this method to shield themselves from giving off too much of their energy or absorbing too much of another person's energy, and when paired with a protective charm it's a wonderful tool to keep negative energies away from you. For my veils, I sew in a specific sigil intended to banish negativity and protect my energy. The veils are either smoke-cleansed or physically washed frequently. I try to wear my banishing veil whenever I leave my home, do a tarot reading for another, or find myself in an emotionally stressful situation. It not only guards my energy but serves as a prerequisite for keeping away energies that would not be beneficial to me.

If you aren't in a position where you can wear a hat or headscarf, you can carry a banishing sigil in your pocket on paper or fabric, or sew it into jeans, shirts, or even hoodies. There are multitudes of banishing methods, and in the coming pages I've listed two of the most basic methods that I personally use. The first, a basic banishing ritual, can be catered to removing either general negative energy or a specific entity. You can even reformulate it as a return to sender spell for baneful magick that has been thrown your way. The second ritual is more specific, and serves as a bath

 to rid your energy of any negativity that someone else has placed on you, like an evil eye, or just to sway a negative energy and person from being in your presence.

# Basic Banishing Ritual

*This banishing ritual can be customized and personalized in any way you see fit—whether that be a return to sender, a specific entity, or negative entity in general. This can be done through tweaking the intention by changing the petition or chant. A return to sender is used to specifically remove the negative energy someone has sent to you (like a hex or malicious energy) and send it back upon the other person. If you are targeting a specific entity, it helps to know the name of the entity, or otherwise be aware of their energy so you know how to target it.*

## MATERIALS:
black candle
piece of paper
fireproof plate
red or black thread (string works as well)

1. Begin this spell by writing out a petition stating what you wish to banish. For petition writing, make sure you write in the present tense—for example, "The negative energy in my space is not welcome" or, "I banish any and all negative entities from my space that wish to do me harm." I like to write out, along with the banishing, "Anyone who directs ill will on me or my hearth receives the ill will returned on to them tenfold."

2. If you wish, write a banishing sigil on the piece of paper with the petition, then fold it away from you.

3. Use the string to wrap around the paper. Make sure you wrap away from you, and continue stating your banishing petition as you do so.

4. On your black candle, you can choose to write a banishing sigil or the banishing petition again. If you cannot use a candle, omit steps 4–5.

5. Seal the banishing petition with wax from the candle, and set underneath the candle as it burns.

6. After the candle has burned down (or you're done with the piece of paper), take the paper and dispose of it outside your house. I prefer to burn my banishing paper in the outdoor fireplace, then scatter the ashes away from my home.

7. Make sure you redo any protection that may have been compromised by the entity.

# A Bath to Banish Negativity

*This spell is best done on a Saturday, or during a waning moon.*

## MATERIALS:
black tea bag
bay leaves
three cloves of garlic
one slice of lemon
basil
sea salt

1. It's best to put these items in some sort of a paper coffee filter or bag to keep them from clogging your drain. I like to tie off my coffee filter with black thread or string.

2. Place each item in and state the intent. I've listed the intent below for each one to help you.

   **BLACK TEA:** intent to protect and banish negativity.
   **BAY LEAVES:** with intent to protect and manifest the spell.
   **THREE CLOVES OF GARLIC:** to ward off evil and negativity.
   **ONE SLICE OF LEMON:** to give those who attempt to place negativity on you a sour taste in their mouths.
   **BASIL:** intent to protect you from harm.

**SEA SALT**: intent to cleanse and purify and remove any negativity that has been placed on you.

3.  After placing each item in and sealing the bag, sit in the bath and imagine the water soaking up all the negativity that has been placed on you. Make sure the water touches every part of your body, including your head, and rinse yourself off after you drain the bath.

Feel free to redo this as often as you like.

# Return to Sender

*A spell to remove any negative energy or ill-intentioned magick that has been thrown your way.*

## MATERIALS:

envelope

salt

hydrangea (optional)

chili peppers or black pepper

piece of paper

thread

1. Take the piece of paper and write on it the following petition or sigil:

   **ANYONE WHO DIRECTS ILL WILL OR NEGATIVE ENERGY TOWARD ME HAS IT RETURNED ON THEM TENFOLD.**

2. Place the piece of paper with your petition on it in the envelope, along with salt, chili peppers or black pepper, and hydrangea, if you have access to it.

3. Take your thread and wrap it around the envelope three times, reciting the following as you do so:

*I am rubber, you are glue,*

*your damage bounces from me back to you.*

*You sent me your hate,*

*Prepare to suffer ten times that fate.*

*My soul is clean, yours is on fire*

*You fucked with a witch*

*Now may the consequences be dire.*

4. After wrapping the envelope, burn completely in a fire-safe area.

5. Dispose of the ashes away from your property.

# BINDING THOSE WHO DO HARM

While banishing is a form of removing a negative energy or entity from a space, binding is a way of ensuring that someone cannot harm you. To bind someone is to wrap them up, metaphysically, and stop all harm and movement they have toward you. Binding can also be done to tie an entity or person to something, like another person, a thought, or even an item. Because of this, I see binding as offensive magick, like banishing, since it's actively working against something that has already taken action against you. Offensive magick can also be described as "second move" magick, where someone has moved the first piece on a chess or checkerboard, and you have to counter their move with your own. Binding is a way to magickally take steps to stop someone from casting against you and causing hurt, and is a vital foundational piece as you begin formulating your practice.

When we consider binding, it's essential to think back to what we discussed at the beginning of the book, and the need to discern whether it is truly necessary, or whether other steps can be taken to ensure your safety in a situation. Would a binding stop your ex from knocking at your door and sending you emails, or would a restraining order be more helpful? Would a binding keep someone away from you and your home, or would an alarm or security system do better? With all forms of magick, we must approach the mundane before the magickal, especially with binding. If you are turning to a binding, it often means that you are worried someone will take action against you or possibly harm you, and I implore you to seek mundane assistance before turning to magick to assist you. Remember that the Craft is a tool, not a solution.

Some typical situations in which I have used a binding are listed below:

✛  To bind someone who had attempted to hex me, paired with a return to sender.

✛  To bind someone to their own jealousy and insecurity.

✛  To bind someone to cease speaking falsehoods about me, paired with a freezer spell—a working done to freeze someone in their tracks.

✛  To bind a spirit to a stone.

✛  To bind someone to stop them from hurting themselves and others.

Although these are among the typical uses for my bindings, there are many others. Some practitioners put bindings in with their banishing spells for specific entities. Some use bindings on anyone they feel is doing them wrong, even if it is not completely true.

There are certain bindings specific to certain needs, and I have used the same basic binding spell for years, customizing it for particular purposes. I've incorporated bindings with banishing spells, protection spells, and to trap bothersome entities. I have always considered bindings to be imperative to the foundation of my craft, and useful in multiple situations.

When incorporating bindings with banishing, I usually bind first in order to make sure the entity doesn't hurt me in the process of the banishing. You can also use a binding jointly with a banishing to get rid of negative energy and people, or even intrusive thoughts when done right. In many cases, bindings can be a form of offensive protection magick—taking a step against someone who has tried to hurt, harm, or do wrong against you in an active way. With binding and banishing, our objective perspective becomes more important than ever. When we are looking to bind someone, we must understand the ramifications of the binding, like all spells, and really look at who we wish to bind. When considering bindings, I ask myself the following questions:

✛ Is the person attempting to harm me or someone I love?

✛ Has this person violated my boundaries and made me feel uncomfortable?

✛ Is this a harmful or malevolent entity that needs to be neutralized?

✛ Will this person respond to conversation?

✛ Would this situation be better handled in a mundane way, such as legal action?

These questions are not to persuade you not to do a binding but rather to make sure you have taken action or put boundaries in place before turning to the spiritual. Bindings are not prone to backfiring, like some offensive magick can sometimes be. However, a binding can, in some instances, backfire in the sense that it doesn't work or on some level the person reacts negatively to it. In some ways, binding could be regarded as domination magick—exerting your will over another to stop them from doing harm to you or another person.

# DOMINATION MAGICK

Domination magick, for the most part, gets a bad reputation due to the ideas of Wicca and the Rule of Three (whatever energy you put into the world is returned to you times three), and most domination magick is perceived as compelling someone to do something. This can be something like compelling the truth, a love spell, pushing someone into therapy, or other methods that are often described as manipulation. In truth, domination magick is extremely helpful to the practitioner. Learning to exert your influence over others can be a foundational part of the Craft, since most aspects of witchcraft are about projecting your influence and will into the world. When we talk about the Craft in general, as we did at the beginning of the book, it's important to understand that all spells have a price. With domination magick, you can sometimes be exerting your will over someone else's will, which is oftentimes seen as problematic by many witches.

When we talk about domination magick, historically, we need to look at who it was created by. Namely, women who depended on men, whether it be husbands, sons, fathers, brothers, for quality of life, or sometimes life in general. Domination magick was created not as a magick of ill intent but rather out of a need for protection by those who had little control over the direction their lives would take. Rarely do we see domination magick praised or used by those with money, power, or privilege, because they need not influence the will of others to receive what they need (Illes, 697–700).

Whether you choose to learn and perform domination magick is up to you, and ultimately your choice is what makes your craft. Since this book leans toward a broad scope of foundational magick for beginners, I will state that learning about domination magick, as a beginner, is important. Performing domination magick, as a beginner, can get trickier depending on the type. For example, bindings rarely backfire, and in that sense are safer for beginners to perform. Truth spells, or spells to receive the truth of a situation, are often considered domination magick, but when done correctly can effectively reveal the information you are seeking without backfiring. A backfire for a truth spell, much like a self-love spell, would be a manifestation in the way you wouldn't expect, or a truth you are not ready to hear. With domination magick, even more so than with other spells, understanding your intent in the situation and examining your will for the spell are imperative.

My questions for you are the following:

✢ In employing domination magick, are you serving your higher good and the higher good of others?

✢ Are you working toward your safety, another's safety, or something they need that they cannot otherwise receive through mundane ways?

✢ Are you casting a love spell on a high school sweetheart because you are *convinced* they are for you and they just don't know it, or an

ex because you feel you have been wronged, or are you casting a love spell for someone who needs love to remain in the home and keep a family together?

✚ Is your domination magick to help the situation overall, however dire, or is it born of petty reasons?

✚ Like all magick, domination magick can be employed to manifest change when used wisely.

# Basic Binding Ritual

*The extra materials listed for this spell are completely optional—*
*all you really need is a black candle, a piece of paper, and string.*
*I tend to use morning glory vines, since my family has some in*
*the summer, and they are often used for binding and banishing.*

## MATERIALS:

morning glory vines

tag lock (this can be a picture, a name, or something like hair
  from the person you want to bind)

string or red thread

black candle

piece of paper

1.  If you wish, you can anoint the black candle with a go
    away oil, or a banishing oil, and carve a sigil for binding.

2.  Light the candle, and write the name of the person on
    the piece of paper, or use their picture.

3.  Fold it away from you once, then fold it away from
    you again.

4. Use the red thread or string to wrap around the folded paper three times, chanting part of the spell below for each wrap:

    *I bind you, (name), from doing harm to me.*
    *I bind you, (name), from doing harm to others.*
    *I bind you, (name), to your actions and their consequences.*

5. After wrapping, tie a knot to begin a witch's ladder, reciting the following after each knot you make. I like to wrap, recite, tie, and then recite, but it really is the practitioner's choice.

    *By knot of ONE, the spell's begun.*
    *By knot of TWO, it cometh true.*
    *By knot of THREE, so mote it be.*
    *By knot of FOUR, the power I store.*
    *By knot of FIVE, the spell's alive.*
    *By knot of SIX, this spell I fix.*
    *By knot of SEVEN, events I'll leaven.*
    *By knot of EIGHT, it will be fate.*
    *By knot of NINE, what's done is mine.*

If you choose to do it my way, the chant would look something like this:

✛ Wrap the string around the folded paper, reciting, "I bind you, (name), from doing harm to me."

✛ Tie a knot, reciting, "By knot of ONE, the spell's begun."

✛ Wrap the string a second time, reciting, "I bind you, (name), from doing harm to others."

✛ Tie a knot, reciting, "By knot of TWO, it cometh true."

✛ Wrap the string a third time, reciting, "I bind you, (name), to your actions and their consequences."

✛ Tie a third knot, reciting, "By knot of THREE, so mote it be."

✛ Wrap the string a fourth time, reciting again, "I bind you, (name), from doing harm to me."

✛ Tie a knot, reciting, "By knot of FOUR, the power I store."

✛ Wrap the string a fifth time, reciting, "I bind you, (name), from doing harm to others."

✛ Tie a knot reciting, "By knot of FIVE, the spell's alive."

✛ Wrap the string a sixth time, reciting, "I bind you, (name), to your actions and their consequences."

✛ Tie a knot reciting, "By knot of SIX, this spell I fix."

✛ Wrap the string a seventh time, reciting, "I bind you, (name), from doing harm to me."

✛ Tie a knot reciting, "By knot of SEVEN, events I'll leaven."

✛ Wrap the string an eighth time, reciting, "I bind you, (name), from doing harm to others."

✛ Tie a knot reciting, "By knot of EIGHT, it will be fate."

✛ Wrap the string for the final, ninth time, reciting, "I bind you, (name), to your actions and their consequences."

✛ Tie a final knot, reciting, "By knot of NINE, what's done is mine."

6. Use wax from the candle to seal the final knot.

7. Place the spell itself in a freezer until you feel the person will not return, or bury it in a place where it will not be dug up.

Disclaimer: A binding spell does not and should not replace assistance from the proper authorities, including the law, in situations where your life may be threatened. Please seek out earthly assistance before turning to the metaphysical.

# You Have No Power Over Me

*This spell is not so much a binding as a charm that is designed to take effect on you to allow someone's words or negativity to affect you less. I like to use this charm to keep my energy confident and strong, which can be especially necessary given my social media presence.*

## MATERIALS:
bowl of water
white candle
rosemary
vanilla extract
cinnamon
thyme
necklace of your choice

1.  Burn the white candle until wax collects.

2.  Set the necklace inside the bowl. Place it in a jar if the necklace cannot be put in water.

3.  Add wax, vanilla, thyme, and cinnamon.

4.  Stirring clockwise, chant: "You have no power over me" as many times as you wish.

5.  Focus your energy on the necklace. If you can visualize, imagine yourself wearing it and the necklace creating an impenetrable white wall of energy around you.

6.  Repeat the charm when needed, and wear the necklace as you please.

# SHADOW WORK +
## AND ITS PURPOSE

*It should be noted that shadow work, as a theory, is based on the archetypes of Carl Jung, who relied primarily on Eastern esoteric philosophical thought to form this psychological theory.*

A lot of practitioners have come to me and asked me how to start shadow work. The real answer is therapy, which presents issues given the lack of affordable mental healthcare in America, as well as the stigmatization of mental health, but to get to the more deeply rooted issues within your shadow self, therapy is important and sometimes necessary. Albeit, not everyone has deeply rooted trauma or childhood wounds but a lot of people do. Many spiritual practitioners will tell you that shadow work can, in some ways, be done without therapy, and they are correct—but it should never take the place of therapy. Shadow work, as a psychological concept, is to be done in conjunction with therapy, never in place of it. You can complete some aspects of shadow work without the help of a licensed mental health professional, and there are many sources for shadow work questions in the form of journals, articles, and workbooks, but learning the coping mechanisms to help you complete shadow work on a daily, continuous basis happens in therapy.

I say this as someone who has had the privilege to be in therapy for an extended period of time: being able to come to terms with certain aspects of my shadow self, as well as ask the more difficult questions, has become much easier after the guidance of a mental health professional. Both repressing the shadow self and learning coping mechanisms to tackle the shadow self are learned behaviors that take time, practice, and active awareness of your energy and shadow self to uncover. Although many list meditation as the first point of shadow work, I tend to journal. When I have an intense response, whether it be based in anger, frustration, or sadness, I write down exactly how I feel and what happened in the situation. From there, I attempt to break down the feeling to understand it better. For instance, I have a habit of taking things personally— when someone says something mean, or in a tone that I interpret as mean, I immediately get upset, defensive, and emotional. When this happened recently, I wrote down the occasion and how it made me feel. From there, I wrote a series of questions:

✙ Why do I pay attention to the negatives more than the positives?

✙ Why do I take people's emotions, especially anger, personally, when I know there is probably something else going on?

✙ Why does it feel like a personal attack?

✙ What can be done to learn and prevent extreme emotional responses to other people's emotions in the future?

These four questions were particular to the situation, what I was feeling, and helped me sort through how to accept the sometimes overly intense emotions that I have. I can be reactive and defensive, an aspect of my shadow self that I have come to terms with, and this played into my questions. After doing shadow work for (technically) the same amount of time I've been a practitioner due to therapy, I've learned how to see past my own ego and quick-fire emotional reactions and break my feelings down to their root cause.

When you are first starting shadow work, I put the importance, especially with my clients and followers, on recognizing when a response feels intense. If you get angry, throw judgment or blame, or have an extreme reaction to a situation that may not warrant that response, the first step is to recognize it. Bringing awareness to our shadow selves, the things we have hidden and hated, is one of the most important parts of working toward acceptance. Being more tolerant of your flaws helps you to be more tolerant of the flaws of others, and offers a new perspective on why they react the way they do. With understanding the shadow self and accepting the shadow self comes healing the shadow self, or, as I lovingly call it, "working with my demons." When I get angry, I don't try to push it away, or rationalize it; instead, I make room for it. I allow myself to be completely and utterly angry without trying to put shame on myself for reacting the way I do, even if I feel like it's an inappropriate or bad reaction. After making space for my emotions, and allowing them to exist without judgment, I often follow a set of questions, similar to the questions above, with the goal of understanding *why I reacted that way* and *where the reaction came from*. Some questions you can start with or adapt to your needs are as follows:

✛ What was the primary emotion your reaction was based in? (Anger, sadness, fear, anxiety.)

✛ What was it about this situation that led to this reaction and feeling in you? Did you feel invalidated by the other person? Did you feel targeted?

✛ Do you feel that by shifting attention to the other person's insecurities or flaws, you are able to successfully avoid something uncomfortable about yourself?

✛ Does the source of this reaction mirror something negative in the past that you experienced? Does it open old wounds, fears, or anxieties?

✛ What is the part of this reaction/situation that is most uncomfortable for you? Why?

✛ How can you hold space for these reactions and emotions in order to further understand them and heal them?

Granted, reaction-based analysis is not the only way to complete shadow work. Many people find meditation, or scheduling time to reflect, beneficial, such as is done in therapy. Using tarot cards is also a great way of completing shadow work, even a more proactive way. Different tarot cards prompt different questions for us to examine based on their meaning. For example, the Devil in the major arcana asks what we willingly chain ourselves to that holds us back, since the Devil represents codependency, addictions, lust, and desire. In the same vein, the High Priestess, famed card of intuition, balance, and mystery, asks us what inner truths we are ignoring. There are many ways to complete this crucial aspect of witchcraft, and the methods stated in this chapter are not the only examples. If another method works for you, pursue it! If you find that the way I complete shadow work is beneficial, it is yours to integrate into your practice.

Looking into our shadow goes beyond understanding how our emotions affect us, and encompasses how they affect the people and world around us, and how our shadow has carried trauma from past generations. Generational trauma is often a topic of conversation around ancestral work and veneration, an important part of many practices. There's a form of ancestral veneration, in some guise or other, in almost every religion and culture in the world. Our shadow, when ignored, does not always affect only us—it can sometimes affect the people around us by continuing cycles of trauma that our ancestors have experienced or by continuing to uphold cycles of oppression that our ancestors created. Through doing shadow work, and facing our flaws and insecurities, the ugliest parts of ourselves become an asset because we understand them. To be a witch is to be constantly learning the ways we can better ourselves, to constantly face our shadows, and learn to work within them.

# Positivity Spell

*This spell is created to keep around the home, and can be done in the form of a large seven-day candle or in the form of a jar. The goal is to shake, place, or light the spell when needing an extra boost of positivity. This is a very versatile spell, and can be formulated and changed depending on the need of the practitioner. If you wish to create this spell for yourself, I recommend a candle or small jar to keep by your bedside. If you wish to create this spell for someone else, I recommend a jar so it may be gifted to them. If you wish to use this spell as a long-term tool to help heal and bring positivity into your life alongside daily mindfulness and action, I recommend both the candle and the jar. Make sure you protect yourself before casting (see page 109 for protection spells).*

## MATERIALS:

jar (with a lid) or white or blue seven-day jar candle

honey (to sweeten your life). Be clear with your intent when you do this. Honey is frequently used in hoodoo for honey jar spells, which can stick a person to you. It's imperative that you use honey with the intent to sweeten a person's life and bring positivity forward. If you are uncomfortable with the use of honey in this spell, it's okay to omit it or use another sweet substance like sugar instead.

lavender (to promote serenity and healing)

rosemary (for protection of home and hearth)

salt (purifying)

bay leaf

three sunflower or fennel seeds

piece of paper (for jar version)

## JAR VERSION

1.  Place the jar in front of you.

2.  Write your intent on the bay leaf, whether that is more positivity in your life, more positivity in someone else's life, or a healing of a situation. Set the bay leaf aside.

3.  Write the name of the person you wish to bring positivity to on the piece of paper. Place in the jar.

4.  Place the other materials in the jar. If you want, visualize bottled happiness. I like to think about what makes me the happiest in that moment and imagine that essence, that feeling, being captured within the jar.

5.  When all materials are in the jar, light the bay leaf and recite the following:

    *Banish negativity,*
    *Bring in the light,*
    *Bring in luck, kindness, and happiness*
    *To the name you contain.*

6.  You may repeat this as many times as you wish, or change the chant to what fits your needs.

7.  Place the ashes and the rest of the bay leaf into the jar and close. If you wish, you can seal the jar with a white candle charged with the same intent or inscribed with a sigil.

8.  Place the jar near a bedside table or where you feel it will be most visible.

## CANDLE VERSION

When doing this version of the spell, imagine that every time the candle is lit, it is letting off positivity or happiness. When the flame flickers, you are sent light. Tapping into specific happy memories and charging the herbs and candle with these feelings of positivity is extremely helpful. Omit the honey|for this version. I recommend creating a sigil to write on the sides of the seven-day candle.

1.  Dig four to five little holes in the candle top and trim the wick.

2.  Write your recipient's name and intent on the bay leaf and set aside.

3.  Place small amounts of herbs into the holes, and make sure not to completely cover the top of the candle to avoid uneven burning.

4.  When finished, light the candle and burn the bay leaf.

**5.** Recite the following:

*Banish negativity,*
*Bring in the light,*
*Bring in luck, kindness, and happiness*
*To the name I burn.*

Like the jar spell, you may repeat this as many times as you wish, or change the chant to what fits your needs.

# PART 4

# UNDERSTANDING OURSELVES AND OUR SHADOW IN A GLOBAL SENSE

# WITCHCRAFT IS A PRACTICE, NOT A RELIGION

**W**itchcraft exists as a practice that dates back thousands of years, and over the centuries has evolved and branched into different paths, forms, and belief sets. No two modern witches follow exactly the same path and the religions of the modern witch range from New Age spirituality all the way to ceremonialism and traditional witchcraft. Some witches are Wiccan, and abide by the Three-fold Law. Some follow the path of Norse paganism or Celtic paganism, and some are atheist. Some witches, like myself, are omnists, and believe that all religions are to an extent valid and should be respected; and some are animists, who believe that all plants, inanimate objects, and natural phenomena hold a soul and a spirit within them. While we discuss the historical bearings of witchcraft, and what it means to be a witch, know that there is room for your belief set or religion to intertwine with your practice. In some spiritual practices, like Thelema, there is no reference to witches, but rather occultists. Many folk magicks and practices would never dare to mention the word "witch," and conduct their spells and prayers in silence. Historically, witchcraft has been a practice to restore and achieve balance within ourselves and the world around us, and has frequently been done in secrecy, oftentimes for safety.

If you ask a passerby witch what it means to be a witch, their answer may totally differ from my answer. Some witch practices may focus on assisting the local community, some may focus on their own spiritual growth and power, and some may focus on communing with higher beings to learn and grow as witches. For some, all of the above. To be a modern witch is to weigh the options in front of you and decide what is best for you. I usually consider it a lot like Robert Frost's poem about roads diverging in a yellow wood, except there are more paths, some well-trodden, some nearly overrun by brambles, and some nonexistent before someone decides to chop through the undergrowth and create something new.

When we talk of more baneful/harmful or offensive magick, we often hear discussion of the Three-fold Law, or certain witches hesitantly pulling away for fear that there will be a backlash distributed by the universe for putting out negative energy. In some witchcraft communities, this difference in morals has been deemed "good" versus "bad," "white" versus "black," or, more recently, "left hand" versus "right hand." In my craft, I refer to this dichotomy as offensive magick and defensive magick. Offensive magick is taking the initiative that represents the divine active aspects of the universe—which could be banishing, hexing, binding, or even healing and undoing. Defensive magick is lying in wait and guarding different aspects of self-protection, self-love, cleansing, or spiritual upkeep, and represents the divine receptive aspects of the universe. The morals of the witch are just that—the morals of the witch. Unless you adhere to the belief set that putting baneful magick into the world will somehow bring harm to you, what type of spells you wish to cast, baneful or not, is totally your business, and not the business of other witches. You'll hear consistent warnings about baneful magick, love spells, and domination magick, which in some situations is that of someone imposing their morals on you, but also a discussion of how these spells are considered more advanced, and therefore more prone to backfiring. My only personal qualm concerning these spells is that it's easy to get wrapped up in the idea of hexes, love spells, and domination magick as a beginner witch, and they can very quickly turn sour against the caster.

It goes without saying that this section discusses concepts that most consider "political." However, I would argue that witchcraft is activism, and always has been activism. Witches have consistently stood up against injustice, fought to right power dynamics, and held the environment in high regard. Spiritual activism is a key to decolonization. I think the importance of witchcraft has always been its role in community affairs, in righting injustices, in preserving the sacred lands of others, in rebalancing power dynamics between the oppressor and the oppressed. When we begin to better ourselves, we can and should consciously look at the world around us and see what we, as those who balance and those who manifest and bring about change, can do to improve it.

It has become, as it has been for decades, the overall occult and pagan community's responsibility to openly denounce white supremacy, decolonize their craft, and make those who hold beliefs that harm others feel uncomfortable in our spaces. Whether you identify as a pagan, if you are reading this chapter, decolonization assists in dismantling white supremacy. Our community, like many other communities, has housed and sheltered hatred by turning a blind eye. When we perhaps fall silent, or stop discussing why these views are inherently harmful—not only to pagan communities but to the overall community of spiritualists, occultists, and witches— there is a chance that white supremacists can find comfort or feel their views have a place here. Historically, occultism was found to have been in use in Nazi Germany (Kurlander, 2015). There are ties to neo-Nazis and Thelemic practices, and most of our occult leaders, like Aleister Crowley, were known nationalists and anti-Semites. As we move forward, as modern witches, there is a responsibility to approach our communities and understand how we have made room for hate, while simultaneously working to remove it for our generation, and future generations.

# WITCHCRAFT AS ACTIVISM

T he root of the word "witch" is from the Old English term *wicca*, meaning a sorcerer, warlock, or male witch, and *wicce*, meaning female witch or sorceress. The first witch trials documented were in 1543 in Denmark, where Gyde Spandemager was accused of casting spells to make the winds fail when Danish ships went after a Dutch fleet. Others include those in 1590 in Scotland, specifically the town of North Berwick, and the Salem witch trials in 1692–93, the most well-known. Whether any of these women were witches or not is open to debate, but the term "witch" has been heavily demonized.

A lot of images of witches may have been linked to anti-Semitic imagery. The *Judenhut* was a cone-shaped hat that Jewish people were forced to wear in certain places in Europe after 1215, and Jewish people were often seen in racist caricatures with the devil's features all echoing the typical characterization of a witch (Shachat, 2020). The idea of witches being persecuted and their image and name being used both for anti-Semitic imagery and propaganda only skims the surface of why witchcraft has always been political.

Religious colonization at the hands of the Christian church reached multiple pagan-dominated communities and, as forced conversion took place, the holidays many pagans celebrated were renamed as Christian holidays. In this Eurocentric colonization, anti-pagan and anti-witch religious decrees were formulated, leading to severe consequences for those who were not Christian. As part of this evangelism, indigenous and First Nations peoples were also targeted when colonization spread to America (Demchak, 2017). Prominent authors in spiritual activism such as Gloria Anzaldúa and Laura E. Pérez discuss spiritual activism and its importance in decolonization, with Pérez exploring the links between imperialism, spirituality, and the ways in which women of color were banished by Eurocentric beliefs. These beliefs centered on civilization, masculinity, and autonomy over animism, which was considered primitive over "respectable" or dominant Eurocentric religions (Keating, 2008). The term "witch" itself is heavily Eurocentric, and outside of Europe other terms were generally used for those who practiced magick.

Apart from people in power using the term "witchcraft" as a way to demonize marginalized groups of people, witchcraft as a practice has always been turned to as a means to bring back control. We can see this in women in the US seeking out witchcraft to soothe anxieties and fears around the 2016 election, in the use of folk magick to heal illness when people were unable to receive proper medical attention, and the rise of interest in spirituality and witchcraft during the Covid-19 pandemic across multiple social media platforms. Some would argue that this surge in interest is a "great awakening," but I would argue it's down to psychology. We turn to the metaphysical when we can't control the mundane, and witchcraft, if anything, is manifesting change in our lives and that of others.

Many facets of the Craft, including traditional witchcraft and folk magick, are earth-based. They put emphasis on connecting with and respecting land spirits. More earth-based religions based around these ideals, like Wicca, Goddess Spirituality, and Neopaganism, which are closely tied to witchcraft, have all evolved from this concept. Animism puts emphasis on each living thing holding a spirit. Witchcraft puts emphasis on working with the elements, and the pentacle, a typical talisman used in witchcraft, embodies this. The use of herbs and crystals and how we source them links directly back to the earth.

Whether practitioners like it or not, witchcraft is political. It has been politicized since the first woman was persecuted as a witch, since the anti-witch laws were used against indigenous and marginalized people, since the image of witches was used as an anti-Semitic trope. "Witch," historically, has been a term for anyone opposed to or conflicting with dominant religions (Sollée, 2020). To be a witch is to stand up against the injustice that witches and those associated with witches have faced for centuries, to fight against colonization, cultural appropriation, and the decimation of the environment.

# WITCHCRAFT AND THE ENVIRONMENT

**W**hen we talk about the environment, we often think of conservationists, scientists, and those who are working within a scientific or biological sphere to take care of the environment. However, our craft and spirituality, in many ways, are historically linked to the earth and its resources. Folk practices are primarily dominated by bio-regionalism—that is, those who practiced only had access to the land and materials around them. While Westernization has led to a materials-centric practice, historically this doesn't align with what the Craft was. The land we live upon is sacred, and many practitioners put emphasis on working with, honoring, or giving respect to the spirits of the land we inhabit. In the twenty-first century, we've noticed dangerous levels of pollution due to the burning of fossil fuels, leading to worldwide concerns on how it's affecting our environment as well as public health. Around 65 percent of the excess mortality rate is attributable to air pollution in multiple countries (Klingmüller, Pozzer, Burnett, Haines, and Ramanathan 2019), and there have been numerous scientific studies showing a direct correlation between fossil fuel combustion, greenhouse gas emissions, and pollution by humans and our all-too-rapidly changing climate, with temperature changes outside of the normal variability documented over the last thousand years (Wuebbles and Jain, 2001). It's no secret that climate change is a real and tangible problem and we must stay alert to the fact that the way we, as humans, consume products creates an unmatchable demand for limited supplies.

As practicing witches, with historical ties to the environment and the land we live upon, it is important for us to understand how and what we take from the earth. While many herbs and crystals can be found easily with major online retailers, I ask you to take a moment and research ethical herb and crystal harvesting. Herbs like white sage and *palo santo* are overharvested to the point where their biodiversity in their natural habitat is threatened; other herbs, like rosemary, garden sage, black sage, and lemon balm, are plants that can be organically sourced and are not at risk in their natural habitats. Rosemary and garden sage are readily available and accessible as cooking herbs in most stores. I even encourage people to research the brands they find in particular stores to make sure they're growing herbs sustainably and ethically, or to grow their own herbs. Some herbs are threatened in specific places, but abundant elsewhere, like arnica—of the thirty-odd accepted species, two are considered endangered: common leopardbane, which is threatened in Florida, Maryland, and Pennsylvania; and heartleaf, which is threatened in Michigan.

And there are issues with the unethical harvesting of many popular crystals—not only are they a non-renewable resource but many of the jobs in the harvesting process are exploitative, associated with extreme human rights violations and environmental harm (Wiseman, 2019). Truth be told, there is no regulation on the crystal industry, and it's often difficult to find businesses that are open to talking about where they source their crystals from.

Just understanding and knowing how to look for ethical and sustainable sources for your herbs and crystals is not only helpful to the environment but helpful to making sure your crystals aren't actively contributing to a practice that is harmful to both people and the land. Looking for sustainable and ethically sourced materials often means seeking out small businesses that are open about where they get their crystals from, or businesses that proudly tout their sustainably sourced herbs. It can be choosing an herb that is local to you and grows in abundance (make sure you check and see the harvesting laws in your country/state), or perhaps growing your own if you have the space. In my practice, I have worked to incorporate herbs that are native to my area or herbs that my ancestors used, to bring me closer to them. Even learning about the environmental ramifications of the overharvesting of white sage and other plants, or researching the social and environmental harms of the crystal industry, is important as a witch. To assist you in starting this journey, here is a quick, general list of endangered or threatened herbs with metaphysical purposes and the areas in which they are considered endangered or threatened. Regardless of where you are based, a quick google should help you make a start in identifying what is endangered in your local area.

## ARNICA

Arnica can be used for enhancing psychic powers. While there are around thirty species of arnica, common leopardbane is endangered in three US states as mentioned previously, and heartleaf in one. Arnica can be purchased as a cultivated or wild-harvested species that is not at risk. Safety note: Please be aware that the overconsumption of arnica can be fatal, and always discuss the use of holistic healing herbs with a doctor first.

## BLACK COHOSH

This herb is listed as endangered in both Illinois and Massachusetts. The demand for black cohosh has resulted in different plants in the genus being overharvested and then classified as endangered, such as mountain bugbane, white baneberry, and Appalachian bugbane, all of which are considered endangered or threatened in separate states due to misidentification by wild harvesters and habitat loss.

## ECHINACEA

There are nine species of echinacea, also known as coneflower or purple coneflower. *Echinacea laevigata*, or smooth purple coneflower, is federally endangered in Pennsylvania. *E. pallida*, or pale purple cornflower, is threatened in both Tennessee and Wisconsin. *E. paradoxa*, or Bush's purple coneflower, is threatened in Arkansas, one of only four states it is found in. *E. purpurea*, or eastern purple coneflower, is endangered in Florida. *E. sanguine*, or sanguine purple coneflower, is threatened in Arkansas. *E. simulata,* or wavyleaf purple coneflower, is threatened in Tennessee. *E. tennesseenis*, or

Tennessee coneflower, is federally endangered, only available in a few counties in that state. The best way to obtain echinacea is to purchase cultivated resources or grow your own.

## WHITE SAGE

Although white sage has no federal protections, it is at risk due to overharvesting. The commercial wild-harvest of *Salvia apiana* is of concern to First Nations groups, conservationists, and herbalists. It is native to only two areas: southwestern California and northwestern Mexico. I don't usually recommend any purchases of white sage because of its overharvesting and because many indigenous groups request those outside of the community not to use it. While indigenous tribes could not practice their traditions or religions until 1978 (when the American Indian Religious Freedom Act was passed), New Age spirituality and occult movements quickly colonized and appropriated the use of the sacred herb for monetary reasons. While many argue "It's just an herb!" and "It belongs to the earth!," the herb, after being stolen for profit by many larger, white companies and organizations, has been overharvested.

## SANDALWOOD

Sandalwood has eight species in the family. All species except for one, *Santalum album*, are native to Hawaii. *S. album* was introduced from India. The habitat of the species in Hawaii is already limited, and both *S. involutum* and *S. freycinetianum* are officially listed as endangered, and both *S. album* and *S. haleakalae* are listed as vulnerable by the International Union for Conservation of Nature. Items like sandalwood oil are not sustainably managed, leading to drastic impacts on the ecology and biosphere of the trees' habitat. A substitute for sandalwood is the wood *Amyris balsamifera,* also known as amyris, and substitutes for sandalwood in incense are benzoin or cedar.

## FRANKINCENSE

Often used for protection, consecration, success, meditation, and in rituals with self, frankincense—obtained from trees of the genus *Boswellia*—represents divinity moving into manifestation. Frankincense resin or oil is often tapped out of the trees in sap form, and the high demand for this substance has created an industry in which as much resin as possible is taken in a short period of time, often leaving the trees damaged (Martinko, 2019). Conservationists advise buyers to look into sustainability at all levels, emphasizing quality over quantity to ensure that *Boswellia* trees are around for longer.

## PALO SANTO

Often used for cleansing but is considered a sacred herb to many indigenous people of South America. There are two trees that yield *palo santo,* "holy wood" in Spanish: *Bursera graveolens* and *Bulnesia sarmientoi.* The latter is endangered in the regions of Argentina, Bolivia, and Paraguay. *Palo santo's* trees are small and slow-growing, so the high demand in the spiritual community has caused the tree *B. sarmientoi* to be listed as endangered by the International Union for Conservation of Nature. *B. graveolens* is considered threatened, but not endangered, by the IUCN. Although some may argue that because only one type of *palo santo* is endangered, it's fine if you source the correct tree, the mere fact of using *palo santo* and contributing to the overharvesting is a disregard for the sacred herb and how it has been used for centuries by indigenous people who, as with white sage, have spoken out against its commodification. Since the time of the Incan empire, the wood has been used for generations by Latinx communities and is considered sacred to them. A few replacements for *palo santo* include dragon's blood, lavender, mugwort, and cedarwood.

## DEVIL'S CLAW ROOT

Native to southern Africa, devil's claw has two species: *Harpagophytum procumbens* and *H. zeyheri.* Devil's claw root is used for protection and to dispel unwanted energies, and can also be used to alleviate rheumatism and other degenerative diseases. Excessive harvesting of the devil's claw, specifically the tubers or roots, has led to severe depletion of the resource. In response, Namibia's Ministry of Agriculture created the Devil's Claw Working Group in 1999 (United Nations University, 2004). Devil's claw is primarily wild-harvested, with around 90 percent of the global supply coming from the wild population in Namibia and the rest from populations in Botswana, Angola, and Zambia. Devil's claw root is used as a traditional medicine by indigenous groups of southern Africa, including the San and Khoikhoi people. Replacements for devil's claw root include mugwort, vervain, and rosemary.

Post-colonization opens up a new dimension to this conversation —if you are located in America, your land belongs to someone else, namely, the First Nations. You can easily look up online what tribe's land you are inhabiting, and pay homage to both the land and the tribe by honoring those who owned it before it was stolen and colonized. When talking about honoring the land, I try to encourage not only opting for sustainably and ethically grown herbs but herbs that have not been bastardized from their sacred use by indigenous peoples and commodified by spiritualists, such as *palo santo* and white sage. Understanding how the land we live upon has been colonized and how sacred herbs have been commodified by practitioners to the detriment of minority communities is an important aspect of examining your impact on the environment as a witch. Honoring the land goes beyond placing offerings out to your favorite tree or being kind to the earth you walk on, but looking to see where you, as a practitioner, can choose an option that is better for the planet. Before buying an herb in bulk, research not only the plant itself and its variety but the supplier. Do they support ethical plant harvesting? Are they transparent with where they get their herbs from and clear with their licensing? When you are buying crystals, are they open with where they source them from? Do they tout their business as ethical and sustainable? These are questions that every practitioner should ask themselves. As we grow as a society, we demand more and more, putting the environment under greater duress. Being mindful of your impact upon the earth is just as imperative in the Craft as learning cleansing or protection.

# DESETTLING AND
# +DECENTERING THE CRAFT

**B**efore we delve into this chapter, it is to be noted that I am in a place of privilege as a white, female presenting individual, and this section will be used primarily to spotlight the historical issues with colonization in the words of Black, indigenous, and Latinx spiritualists, as well as to bring attention to their voices and works as resources on further decentering your craft. It is imperative, then, when we discuss decolonization of spirituality, that we center the voices of people of color.

In order to understand the colonization of spirituality and witchcraft, it's important to define a few terms that will be used frequently throughout this chapter:

✛ *Colonization*, noun, (1) the action or process of settling among and establishing control over the indigenous people of an area; (2) the action of appropriating a place or domain for one's own use.

✛ *Cultural appropriation,* noun, the unacknowledged or inappropriate adoption of the customs, practices, ideas, etc., of one people or society by members of another and typically more dominant people or society.

✛ *Closed practice* is defined as any tradition that requires initiation or a specific teaching in order to be brought into the tradition. A closed practice is also one where the way it is taught is passed down within families or part of a specific culture. A few practices by initiation include Wicca and vodou, and a few practices where it is passed down within families or mentors is *hoodoo,* Italian folk magick, and Irish/Celtic folk magick. An example of a closed practice of a specific culture is indigenous spiritualities and *brujería.*

✛ *Open practice* is defined as a practice or tradition that is open to individuals from other cultures and does not require initiation.

✛ *Decolonization* refers to the work of those who have been colonized to remove the effects of colonization from their practice.

✛ *Desettling* and *decentering* refer to the work of those who are white to recenter indigenous and Black voices while decentering white narratives around topics of anti-racism, colonization, and cultural appropriation. While these are important topics for anti-racist and settler allies to learn about, the teachings and voices of people of color (POC) within our community, especially those that have been strongly affected by colonization, must be given greater prominence than white voices when we discuss desettling and decentering as an adjacent work to decolonization.

When we talk about decentering, desettling, and decolonization we are discussing terms and ideas that have many different theoretical approaches, and this part will center primarily around a womanist/ feminist point of view. You'll often find that academic articles avoid conversations about spiritual activism and decolonizing spirituality. Laura E. Pérez states that this is a legacy of colonialism due to the idea that Western ideals prioritize white, male logic over spirituality, often viewed as superstition and folk belief. Within this sphere, women of color are the most ignored, especially by white spiritualists.

If you spend any time within spiritual spaces, both on and offline, you may note arguments over closed practices and cultural appropriation. You'll also find discussions about minority-dominated spiritual paths and religions, what cultural appropriation is or isn't, and what many people think about it. When we discuss cultural appropriation, like colonization, we have to keep POC in the center of the conversation. Therefore, I will only be discussing culturally appropriative items that have been raised by Black, indigenous, and Latinx spiritualists in public spheres. Some of the most commonly discussed spiritual items are white sage and *palo santo*. Ruth Hopkins, a Lakota/Sioux writer, describes the harm that the appropriation of white sage has done as "exploitative . . . amounts to silencing Native voices and erasing our cultural heritage" (Burton and Polish, 2021). In the same vein, *palo santo* has been harvested to the point where many indigenous groups in South America are losing access to a sacred plant, considered "holy wood," that they have used for generations longer than any white practitioner. Making sure your craft doesn't infringe on other cultures, or appropriate them, is merely the tip of the iceberg to desettling your craft.

Decentering and desettling is the process of changing the narrative around white imperialism and disrupting the role colonization has played, primarily at the hands of the Eurocentric world. When we live in the Western world, most of what we see is a product of colonization. Almost everything we read is a byproduct of colonization and derives from a Eurocentric mindset. Decentering and desettling your craft is not just avoiding closed practices and cultural appropriation but looking at the historical ramifications of colonization, listening to and learning from POC on their terms, as well as taking research into your own hands. Decolonization of your craft requires decolonization of your mindset—to see things beyond the Western world, whiteness, gender, patriarchy, and Eurocentricity. If you are white and raised in the West, I assure you that you have already been indoctrinated into what is called the "colonizer mindset." This isn't something to be embarrassed or defensive about. It's simply a matter of fact. What matters is what you do to change that—do you continue ignoring the issues the world and marginalized groups are facing from a position of privilege, or do you begin dismantling the mindset you were born into? How do you desettle? While this chapter, as with elsewhere in this book, provides you with a spell you can use, I also want to prioritize and emphasize amazing POC activists, theorists, and writers for you to learn from.

Following is a list of books and papers to help you begin your decentering and desettling work, but it doesn't stop there—you will continually be unpacking racist and colonized notions, thought processes, and mindsets as a person of privilege. You, as a witch, will always be learning. I am still learning. It is your responsibility, if you are a person of privilege, to unpack ingrained ideas and falsehoods, to continuously learn, and be more mindful of your actions as a person and as a witch.

*The New Jim Crow* by Michelle Alexander
*How to Be an Antiracist* by Ibram X. Kendi
*The White Possessive: Property, Power, and Indigenous Sovereignty* by
     Aileen Moreton-Robinson
*Decolonizing Methodologies: Research and Indigenous Peoples*
     by Linda Tuhiwai Smith
*Witchcraft as Political Resistance* by Sabina Magliocco
*Chicana Art: The Politics of Spiritual and Aesthetic Altarities*
     by Laura E. Pérez
*Borderlands/La Frontera* by Gloria Anzaldúa
*Decolonizing the Spirit in Education and Beyond* edited
     by Njoki Nathani Wane
*Bringing Race to the Table: Exploring Racism in Pagan*
     *Communities* by Crystal Blanton

Some practitioners and spiritualists may argue that decentering and desettling is unnecessary. That it's creating boundaries when we are one human race, and that our souls have no race or culture. Or that spirituality is about looking inward and activism is about looking outward. The spiritualists who take this stance are often coming from a place of privilege and have not faced the destruction of their culture as a result of colonization and cultural appropriation. When we look at our shadow, we have to look past it, to how our actions affect the world around us, especially marginalized communities when we are coming from a place of privilege. Desettling and decentering are important because silence and complacency only continue the cycle of colonization and therefore perpetuate a cycle of harm.

In the same vein, some practitioners would argue that witchcraft of all kinds is so heavily stolen or appropriated from so many different places, that the blurring of lineage makes it okay to practice what you want. What this kind of mindset often ignores is the narrative of the oppressed: those who were enslaved from the continent of Africa who were forcibly transported to this land, bringing with them various traditional religions and practices from which evolved hoodoo. These practitioners still face systematic oppression by way of the entire US system to this day. Indigenous lands that were aggressively colonized by English settlers, displacing Native Americans and blocking them from practicing their sacred rites and rituals by law until the American Indian Religious Freedom Act of 1978. Witchcraft and practices of witchcraft, including folk magick (although indigenous rituals and hoodoo are not considered witchcraft by Native and Black individuals), were heavily demonized by white colonizers in their homelands, which then transferred over to America when they immigrated. Only when the 1970s birthed the dawn of the New Age of spirituality did sage and "smudging," psychics who could tell your fortune, and cards that could read your future, become a mainstream idea. I am not asking you not to practice modern-day witchcraft, which is heavily colonized in many respects, but rather to be aware of the origins of your own practice as you begin to formulate it, and to be conscious of how colonization has given white spirituality and Western esoteric thought space to exist and steal from minority groups.

Anzaldúa's spiritual activism elicits the epitome of manifesting change with witchcraft. It brings forth ideas of spirituality for the betterment of society, using witchcraft to heal and transform not just our own world but the world as a whole (Keating, 2008). When we build our foundation for the Craft, we are building it not just for ourselves but for the greater community of witches and spiritualists, including the ones who have been affected by colonization.

# Justice Spell

*A spell to assist in a situation in which the victim has not received the justice they deserve by law enforcement or the legal system.*

## MATERIALS:
purple prayer candle or votive candle
calendula flowers
oregano
eggshells
chili
clove or cinnamon oil

1. Use a mortar and pestle to grind together the herbs and other dry items to get a slightly fine powder.

2. Anoint the candle with an oil and roll it in the herb powder, or place the powder on top of the prayer candle. Make sure to apply the powder lightly to avoid excess powder becoming a fire hazard.

3. Leave on your altar overnight atop your petition for justice, a sigil, or the Justice tarot card. If you own kyanite, you can also keep that nearby to charge the spell. An example of a petition is:

*An injustice has been caused, through ignorance or malice, and this injustice has caused the damage and/or death of others. I humbly ask you (the universe, ancestors, deities, etc.) to guide my hand, to push my will forward, to seek justice for (list names of those seeking justice) against (who committed the injustice) in (place of injustice, where the person lives, etc.), in whatever way you see fit.*

4.  Before lighting the candle, cast a circle. If you wish to invoke a certain energy, deity, or ancestor to assist you, you may do so.

5.  Prop the tarot card of Justice before you and light the candle. Burn the petition and meditate on your intent and goal of the spell.

*Allow the candle to burn until it is finished, or continue working the spell throughout the week by lighting it, meditating on it, then putting it out if need be. For my seven-day candle spells, I light them in the morning and let them go until night. Keep the candle around the Justice card as it is burning, and continue pushing for justice through mundane ways as well (signing petitions, donating, protesting, depending on the cause you are working toward).*

# AFTERWORD

As this book draws to a close and the words I can think to write down dwindle, I'm left with, very simply, what I originally wanted to create with *Spells for Change*—a book that I didn't have when I began practicing, that summarizes how we can build a foundation for our craft and which prioritizes both the personal and the communal. My hope is that this book will show you that all witches are different in their walks of life, and no practice will look the same as another practice. I hope this book shows how witchcraft has functioned as a way of life and a way of transformation for decades, and that it inspires you to choose change moving forward. While witchcraft can be both solitary and community-based, our choices concerning how we approach the world can be filled with compassion for those around us and the land itself. What you choose to do with this book past these pages is beyond my control, though I hope it continues to be a valuable resource for those beginning their path, or even those who are looking for a new perspective.

# BIBLIOGRAPHY AND SUGGESTED READING

Although this book is written primarily from my own experiences and the information that I have collected from my own studies on witchcraft, I have created a suggested reading list. It contains books I used to help research this book, other beginner books, and books that I consider to be the next stepping-stone in learning about witchcraft.

## BOOKS

Pasi, Marco: *Aleister Crowley and the Temptation of Politics* (New York: Routledge, 2014)

*The Bhagavad Gita,* translated by Patton, L. (London: Penguin, 2014)

Blanton, Ellwood, Williams, Crystal, Taylor, Brandy: *Bringing Race to the Table: Exploring Racism in the Pagan Community* (Megalithica, 2015)

Hine, Phil: *Condensed Chaos: An Introduction to Chaos Magic* (Arizona: The Original Falcon Press, 1995)

Cunningham, Scott: *Cunningham's Book of Shadows: The Path of the American Traditionalist* (Minnesota: Llewellyn, 2009)

Om, Mya: *Energy Essentials for Witches and Spellcasters* (Minnesota: Llewellyn, 2009)

Dunwich, Gerina: *Herbal Magick* (Massachusetts: Weiser, 2019)

Vaudoise, Mallorie: *Honoring Your Ancestors: A Guide to Ancestral Veneration* (Minnesota: Llewellyn, 2019)

Miller, Jason: *Protection and Reversal Magick* (New Jersey: The Career Press, 2006)

Auryn, Mat: *Psychic Witch* (Minnesota: Llewellyn, 2020)

Jung, Carl: *Psychology and Religion: West and East* (New Jersey: Princeton University Press, 1969)

Zakroff, Laura Tempest: *Sigil Witchery* (Minnesota: Llewellyn, 2018)

Wachter, Aidan: *Six Ways: Approaches and Entries for Practical Magic* (Red Temple Press, 2018)

Pérez, Laura E.: *Chicana Art: The Politics of Spiritual and Aesthetic Altarities* (North Carolina: Duke University Press, 2007)

Illes, Judika: *The Encyclopedia of 5000 Spells* (New York: HarperCollins, 2009)

Roséan, Lexa: *The Encyclopedia of Magickal Ingredients: A Wiccan Guide to Spellcasting* (New York: Pocket Books, 2005)

Hall, Manly P.: *The Secret Teachings of All Ages* (San Francisco: H. S. Crocker Company, Inc 2007)

Cantin, Tierra, Candis, Michael: *The Spirit of Herbs: A Guide to the Herbal Tarot* (Stamford: U.S. Game Systems, 1993)

Oerter, Robert: *The Theory of Almost Everything* (New York: Pearson Education, 2006)

Gary, Gemma: *Traditional Witchcraft: A Cornish Book of Ways* (Cornwall: Troy Books, 2008)

Zakroff, Laura Tempest: *Weave the Liminal: Living Modern Traditional Witchcraft* (Minnesota: Llewellyn 2019)

Sollée, Kristen J.: *Witch Hunt: A Traveler's Guide to the Power and Persecution of the Witch* (Massachusetts: Weiser Books, 2020)

Alden, Temperance: *Year of the Witch: Connecting with Nature's Seasons* (Massachusetts: Weister Books, 2020)

## OTHER SOURCES

Magliocco, Sabina, 2020. Witchcraft as Political Resistance. Nova Religio, 23(4), pp.43–68.

Kurlander, Eric, 2015. The Nazi Magicians' Controversy: Enlightenment, "Border Science," and Occultism in the Third Reich. *Central European History*, 48(4), pp.498–522.

Keating, AnaLouise, 2008. "I'm a Citizen of the Universe": Gloria Anzaldúa's Spiritual Activism as Catalyst for Social Change. *Feminist Studies*, 34(1/2), pp.53–69.

Lelieveld, J., Klingmüller, K., Pozzer, A., Burnett, R., Haines, A. and Ramanathan, V., 2019. Effects of fossil fuel and total anthropogenic emission removal on public health and climate. *Proceedings of the National Academy of Sciences*, 116(15), pp.7192–7197.

Wuebbles, Donald J. and Jain, Atul, 2001. Concerns about climate change and the role of fossil fuel use. *Fuel Processing Technology*, 71(1-3), pp.99–119.

Martinko, Katherine, 2019. Frankincense Is Endangered. *Treehugger*. https://www.treehugger.com/frankincense-endangered-4855261 [Accessed 9 August 2021]

Engels, Gayle and Brinckmann, Josef, 2018. Devil's Claw Harpagophytum procumbens, H. zeyheri Family: Pedaliaceae. *HerbalGram*, (118), pp.8–14.

Fortier, Craig, 2017. Unsettling Methodologies/Decolonizing Movements. *Journal of Indigenous Social Development*, 6(1), pp.20–36.

International Gem Society. https://www.gemsociety.org/
[Accessed 9 August 2021].

Shachat, Emma, 2020. The Antisemitic History of Witches. *Alma*.
https://www.heyalma.com/the-antisemitic-history-of-witches/
[Accessed 9 August 2021]

Wiseman, Eva, 2019. Are crystals the new blood diamonds?. *The
Guardian*. https://www.theguardian.com/global/2019/jun/16/are-
crystals-the-new-blood-diamonds-the-truth-about-muky-business-
of-healing-stones [Accessed 9 August 2021]

Burton, Nylah and Polish, Jay, 2019. The Ethics Of Burning Sage,
Explained. *Bustle*. https://www.bustle.com/wellness/is-burning-sage-
cultural-appropriation-heres-how-to-smoke-cleanse-in-sensitive-
ways-18208360 [Accessed 9 August 2021]

# ACKNOWLEDGMENTS

This book wouldn't have been possible without a number of people. Thank you firstly to my editor, Zoe Yang, who has been an enormous support with helping me find structure. To my parents, to whom the book is dedicated, thank you for continuing to inspire me to incite change, push the envelope, and for nurturing my voice and spirit from a young age. Thank you to my peers, namely Robyn, Temperance, Nike, Georgina, and Anne, who gave me friendship, kindness, and community. Thank you to Omi, Honey, Owen, and Kat Borealis, who have helped me approach my topics with care and never cease to amaze me. Thank you to my assistant, Ashley, who quite literally keeps me sane and gave me enough leeway to make this book. Thank you to my friends—Honey, Savannah, Matt, Emma, Liv, L, Quiiroi, Persie, Mama Bones, Eoin, and Omi, who have consistently shown me support in all my crazy endeavors. Thanks to my younger sisters who simultaneously stress me out and impress me daily. In true pagan fashion, I also give thanks to my Divine guides. Thank you to my ancestors, my patron deities, Freyja, Lady Diana, Lord Luciferos, my familiar, Vulpes, and my plant and animal allies for protecting and guiding me on my path.

# ABOUT THE AUTHOR

Frankie Anne Castanea is a practicing neopagan and eclectic/ folk witch of six years. She is more commonly known as Chaotic Witch Aunt on the internet, and you can find her on Instagram, YouTube, and TikTok under that name where she has over a million followers, runs a tarot reading business, and creates both comedic and educational content. She has been interviewed by *Nylon* and *Bust* to discuss her online community. This is her debut book.